URBAN
TRAILS
KITSAP

URBAN
TRAILS
KITSAP

**Bainbridge Island · Key Peninsula
Bremerton/Silverdale · Gig Harbor**

CRAIG ROMANO

MOUNTAINEERS
BOOKS

MOUNTAINEERS BOOKS

Mountaineers Books is the publishing division of The Mountaineers, an organization founded in 1906 and dedicated to the exploration, preservation, and enjoyment of outdoor and wilderness areas.

1001 SW Klickitat Way, Suite 201, Seattle, WA 98134
800.553.4453, www.mountaineersbooks.org

Printed in China
Distributed in the United Kingdom by Cordee, www.cordee.co.uk
First edition: first printing 2016, second printing 2017, third printing 2018

Copy Editor: Jane Crosen
Design and Layout: Jen Grable
Cartographer: Lohnes + Wright
All photographs by author unless otherwise noted.
Cover photo: *View from Fort Ward Park across Rich Passage*
Frontispiece: *Signage at Twanoh Creek*

Library of Congress Cataloging-in-Publication Data on file

ISBN (paperback): 978-1-68051-022-5
ISBN (ebook): 978-1-68051-023-2

A Note about Safety: Safety is an important concern in all outdoor activities. No guidebook can alert you to every hazard or anticipate the limitations of every reader. Therefore, the descriptions of roads, trails, routes, and natural features in this book are not representations that a particular place or excursion will be safe for your party. When you follow any of the routes described in this book, you assume responsibility for your own safety. Under normal conditions, such excursions require the usual attention to traffic, road and trail conditions, weather, terrain, the capabilities of your party, and other factors. Keeping informed on current conditions and exercising common sense are the keys to a safe, enjoyable outing. —Mountaineers Books

CONTENTS

BAINBRIDGE ISLAND

TRAIL LOCATOR MAP

101

Whidbey
Island

Hansville
29 27 28

101   104

Port
Gamble

26

Olympic
National
Forest

3

Kingston

Edmonds

25

Poulsbo
24

305   36

Puget
Sound

3

5

Hood
Canal

35

Silverdale   34

22   17   33   Bainbridge
303   32   Island

Seabeck   20   16   31   Seattle

15   30

18
19   14

23   Bremerton

21

Kitsap Peninsula

Port
Orchard

160   Southworth

101

3   13   16   10

Belfair

300   12   9   Vashon
Island

2   1   Purdy

106   11   302

8   Gig
5   6   Harbor
3   7

3   Key
Peninsula

4

16

5

Tacoma

Shelton

512

N

0   10 miles

101

DuPont

TRAILS AT A GLANCE

Trail and/or Park	Distance	Walk	Hike	Run	Kids	Dogs
KEY PENINSULA						
1. 360 Trails	More than 8 miles of trails	•		•	•	•
2. Rocky Creek Conservation Area	More than 3 miles of trails		•	•	•	•
3. Maple Hollow Park	1 mile round-trip		•		•	•
4. Penrose Point State Park	2.5 miles of trails	•	•		•	•
KITSAP PENINSULA						
5. McCormick Forest	4 miles of trails		•	•	•	•
6. Rotary Bark Park	3 miles of trails	•	•	•	•	•
7. Sehmel Homestead Park	4 miles of trails	•	•	•	•	•
8. Cushman Powerline Trail	6.2 miles one-way	•		•	•	•
9. Anderson Point Trail	1.4 miles round-trip	•	•		•	•
10. Banner Forest Heritage Park	29 miles of trails		•	•	•	•
11. Twanoh Creek Loop	2.3 miles round-trip		•	•	•	•
12. Theler Wetlands	3 miles of trails	•	•		•	
13. Square Lake	1 mile round-trip		•			•
14. Manchester State Park	1.9 miles of trails	•	•		•	•
15. Lions Park and Stephenson Canyon	2.4 miles of trails	•	•	•	•	•
16. Illahee Preserve Heritage Park	5 miles of trails		•	•	•	•
17. Clear Creek Trail	More than 7 miles of trails	•		•	•	•

Trail and/or Park	Distance	Walk	Hike	Run	Kids	Dogs
18. Big Tree Trail	1.4 miles round-trip		•		•	
19. Ueland Tree Farm	0.8 mile trail/more than 14 miles woods roads	•	•	•	•	•
20. Newberry Hill Heritage Park	12 miles of trails		•	•	•	•
21. Green Mountain	5.2 miles round-trip		•	•		•
22. Anderson Landing Preserve	2 miles of trails		•			•
23. Guillemot Cove Nature Reserve	4 miles of trails		•		•	
24. Poulsbo's Fish Park	1.5 miles of trails	•			•	•
25. North Kitsap Heritage Park	More than 10 miles of trails	•	•	•	•	•
26. Port Gamble Trails	More than 60 miles of trails and woods roads	•	•	•	•	•
27. Hansville Greenway	More than 8 miles of trails	•	•	•	•	•
28. Point No Point	0.8 mile of trail and nearly 1.5 miles of beach	•	•		•	•
29. Foulweather Bluff	1.9 miles round-trip	•	•		•	
BAINBRIDGE ISLAND						
30. Fort Ward Park	2 miles round-trip	•	•	•	•	•
31. Gazzam Lake Nature Preserve	4 miles of trails		•	•	•	•
32. Pritchard Park	1.2 miles round-trip	•			•	•
33. Grand Forest Park	8 miles of trails		•	•	•	•
34. Battle Point Park Loop	1.6 miles round-trip	•			•	•
35. Manzanita Trails	2 miles of trails		•	•		•
36. West Port Madison Nature Trail	0.6 mile round-trip	•			•	•

INTRODUCTION
TRAILS FOR FUN AND FITNESS IN YOUR BIG BACKYARD

LET'S FACE IT: WHETHER YOU'RE a hiker, walker, or runner, life can get in the way when it comes to putting time in on the trail. Far too often, it's hard for most of us to set aside an hour—never mind a day, or even longer—to hit the trails of our favorite parks and forests strewn across the state. But that doesn't mean we can't get out on the trail more frequently. Right in our own communities are thousands of acres of parks and nature preserves containing hundreds of miles of trails. And we can visit these pocket wildernesses, urban and urban-fringe parks and preserves, greenbelts, and trail corridors on a whim—for an hour or two without having to drive far. Some of these places we can even visit without driving at all—hopping on our bikes or the bus instead—lessening our carbon footprint while giving us more time to relax from our hurried schedules.

Urban Trails: Kitsap focuses on the myriad of trails, parks, and preserves within the urban and suburban areas around Bremerton, Silverdale, Bainbridge Island, Gig Harbor, and the Key and Kitsap peninsulas. You'll find trails to beaches, old-growth forests, lakeshores, wildlife-rich wetlands, rolling hills, scenic vistas, meadows, historic sites, and vibrant communities. While often we equate hiking trails with the state's wildernesses and forests, there are plenty of areas of natural beauty and accessible trails in the midst of our population centers. The routes included here are designed to show you where you can go for a nice run, long walk, or quick hike right in your own backyard.

This guide has two missions. One is to promote fitness and get you outside more often! A trip to Mount Rainier, North Cascades, or Olympic national parks can be a major undertaking for many of us. But a quick outdoor getaway to a local park or trail can be done almost anytime—before work, during a lunch break, after work, or when we don't feel like fighting traffic and driving for miles. And most of these trails are available year round, so you can walk, run, or hike every day. If you feel you are not getting outside enough or getting enough exercise, this book can help you achieve a healthier lifestyle.

Mission number two of this guide is to promote the local parks, preserves, and trails that exist within our urban areas. More than four million people (60 percent of the state's population) call the greater Puget Sound home. While conservationists continue to promote protection of our state's large roadless wild corners—and that is still important—it's equally important that we promote the preservation of natural areas and develop more trails and greenbelts right where

Story wall at the Japanese-American Exclusion Memorial at Pritchard Park

Washington's state flower, the Pacific rhododendron, grows in profusion around the Kitsap Peninsula.

people live. Why? For one thing, the Puget Sound area contains unique and threatened ecosystems that deserve to be protected as much as our wilder remote places. And, we need to have usable and accessible trails where people live, work, and spend the majority of their time. Urban trails and parks allow folks to bond with nature and be outside on a regular basis. They help us cut our carbon footprint by giving us access to recreation without burning excessive gallons of fuel to reach a destination. They make it easier for us to commit to regular exercise programs, giving us safe and agreeable places to walk, run, and hike. And urban trails and parks also offer for disadvantaged populations—folks who may not have cars and/or the means to travel to one of our national parks or forests—a chance to experience nature and a healthy lifestyle too. As our urban areas continue to grow, it is all the more important that we support the expansion of our urban parks and trails.

So get out there, get fit, and have fun!

HOW TO USE
THIS GUIDE

THIS EASY-TO-USE GUIDE PROVIDES YOU with enough details to get out on the trail with confidence, while leaving enough room for your own personal discovery. I have walked, hiked, and/or run every mile of trails described here, and the directions and advice are accurate and up to date. Conditions can and do change, however, so make sure you check on the status of a park or trail before you go.

THE ROUTES

This book includes thirty-six routes, or park trail systems, covering trails on the Key Peninsula, Kitsap Peninsula, and Bainbridge Island. Each one begins with the park and/or trail name followed by the agency responsible for managing it. Next is a block of information detailing the following:

Distance. Here you will find round-trip mileage (unless otherwise noted) if the route describes a single trail; or the total mileage of trails within the park/preserve/greenway if the route gives an overview of the destination's trail system. Note that while I have measured most of the trails in this book with GPS and have consulted maps and governing land agencies, the distance stated may not always be exact—but it'll be pretty darn close.

Elevation gain. For individual trails, elevation gain is for the *cumulative* difference on the route (and return), meaning not only the difference between the high and low points on the trail, but also for all other significant changes in elevation along the way. For destinations where multiple routes are given, as in a trail network within a park, the elevation gain applies to the steepest trail on the route.

High point. The high point is the highest elevation of the trail or trail system described. Almost all of the trails in the book are at a relatively low elevation, assuring mostly snow-free winter access.

Difficulty. This factor is based not only on length and elevation gain of a trail or trails, but also on the type of tread and surface area of the trail(s). Most of the trails in this book are easy or moderate for the average hiker/walker/runner. Depending on your level of fitness, you may find the trails more or less difficult than described.

Fitness. This description denotes whether the trail is best for hikers, walkers, or runners. Generally, paved trails will be of more interest to walkers and runners, while rough, hilly trails will appeal more to hikers. Of course you are free to hike, walk, or run (unless park regulations specifically prohibit running) any of the trails in this book.

Family-friendly. Here you'll find notes on a trail's or park's suitability for children and any cautions to be aware of such as cliffs, heavy mountain bike use, etc. Some trails may be noted as suitable for jogging strollers and ADA-accessible.

Dog-friendly. This denotes whether dogs are allowed on the trail and what regulations (such as leashed and under control) apply.

Amenities. The featured park's amenities can include privies, drinking water, benches, interpretive signs/displays, shelters, learning centers, campgrounds, and doggy-bag dispensers, to name a few.

A close encounter at Close Beach (Gazzam Lake Nature Preserve)

Contact/map. Here you'll find contact info for where to get current trail conditions, including websites and phone numbers for trail and park managers or governing agencies. These websites will often direct you to trail and park maps, and in some cases, a better or supplemental map is noted (such as Green Trails).

GPS. GPS coordinates are provided for the main trailhead, to help get you to the trail.

Before You Go. This section notes any fees or permits required, hours the park or preserve is open (if limited), closures, and any other special concerns.

Next I describe how to get to the trailhead via your own vehicle or by public transport if the trail is served by this mode.

GETTING THERE. Driving: provides directions to the trailhead—generally from the nearest large town and often from more than one direction—and also parking information.

Transit: If the trailhead is served by public transportation, this identifies the bus agency and line, and the stop location.

EACH HIKE begins with an overview of the featured park and/or trail, highlighting its setting and character, with notes on the property's conservation history.

GET MOVING. This section describes the route or trails and what you might find on your hike, walk, or run, and may note additional highlights beyond the trail itself, such as points of historical interest.

GO FARTHER. Here you'll find suggestions for making your hike/walk/run longer within the featured park—or perhaps by combining this trip with an adjacent park or trail.

PERMITS, REGULATIONS, AND PARK FEES

Most of the trails and parks described in this book are managed by county and city parks departments, requiring no permits or fees. Destinations managed by Washington State Parks and the Washington Department of Natural Resources (DNR) require a day-use fee in the form of the Discover Pass (www.discoverpass.wa.gov) for vehicle access. A Discover Pass costs $10 per vehicle per day or $30 for up to two vehicles annually. You can purchase the pass online, at many retail outlets, or better yet, from a state park office to avoid the $5 handling fee. Each hike in this book clearly states if a fee is charged or a pass is required.

Regulations such as whether dogs are allowed, a park has restricted hours, or is closed for certain occasions (such as during high fire danger) are clearly spelled out in each trail's information block.

ROAD AND TRAIL CONDITIONS

In general, trails change little year to year. But change can and does occur, and sometimes very quickly. A heavy storm can wash out sections of trail or access road in moments. Wind storms can blow down trees across trails by the hundreds, making paths unhikable. Lack of adequate funding is also responsible for trail neglect and degradation. On some of the wilder destinations in this book, it is wise to contact the appropriate land manager after a significant weather event to check on current trail and road conditions.

On the topic of trail conditions, it is vital that we acknowledge the countless volunteers who donate tens of thousands of hours to trail maintenance each year. The Washington Trails Association (WTA) alone coordinates upwards of one hundred thousand hours of volunteer trail maintenance each year. But, there is always a need for more. Our trail system faces ever-increasing threats, including lack of adequate trail funding. Consider joining one or more of the trail and conservation groups listed in the Resources.

OUTDOOR ETHICS

A strong, positive outdoors ethic includes making sure you leave the trail (and park) in as good or even better condition than you found it. Get involved with groups and organizations that safeguard, watchdog, and advocate for land protection. And get on the phone and keyboard, and let land managers and public officials know how important protecting lands and trails is to you.

All of us who recreate in Washington's natural areas have a moral obligation and responsibility to respect and protect our natural heritage. Everything we do on the planet has an impact—and we should strive to have as minimal negative impact as possible. The **Leave No Trace** Center for Outdoors Ethics is an educational, non-partisan nonprofit organization that was developed for responsible enjoyment and active stewardship of the outdoors. Their program helps educate outdoor enthusiasts of their recreational impacts and recommends techniques to prevent and minimize such impacts. While geared toward backcountry use, many Leave No Trace (LNT) principles are also sound advice for urban and urban

A solid boardwalk through a Port Gamble Trail wetland area assures dry and mud-free hiking shoes.

fringe parks too, including: plan ahead, dispose of waste properly, and be considerate of other visitors.

TRAIL ETIQUETTE

We need to be sensitive not only to the environment surrounding our trails, but to other trail users as well. Some of the trails in this book are also open to mountain bikers and equestrians.

When you encounter other trail users, whether they are hikers, runners, bicyclists, or horse riders, the only hard-and-fast rule is to follow common sense and exercise simple courtesy. With this Golden Rule of Trail Etiquette firmly in mind, here are other things you can do during trail encounters to make everyone's trip more enjoyable:

- **Right-of-way.** When meeting bicyclists or horseback riders, those of us on foot should move off the trail. This is because hikers, walkers, and runners are more mobile and flexible than other users, making it easier for us to step off the trail.

- **Encountering horses.** When meeting horseback riders specifically, step off the downhill side of the trail unless the terrain makes this difficult or dangerous. In that case, move to the uphill side of the trail, but crouch down a bit so you do not tower over the horses' heads. Also, make yourself visible so as not to spook the big beastie, and talk in a normal voice to the riders. This calms the horses. If walking with a dog, keep your buddy under control.
- **Stay on trails.** Don't cut switchbacks, take shortcuts, or make new trails; all lead to erosion and unsightly trail degradation.
- **Obey the rules specific to the trail or park you are visiting.** Many trails are closed to certain types of use, including dogs and mountain bikes.
- **Hiking, walking, or running with dogs.** Trail users who bring dogs should have their dog on a leash or under very strict voice-command at all times. And if leashes are required, then this DOES apply to you. Many trail users who have had negative encounters with dogs (actually the dog owners) on the trail are not fond of, or are even afraid of, encountering dogs. Respect their right *not* to be approached by your darling pooch. A well-behaved leashed dog, however, can certainly help warm up these folks to a canine encounter.
- **Avoid disturbing wildlife.** Observe from a distance, resisting the urge to move closer to wildlife (use your binoculars or telephoto lens). This not only keeps you safer, but it prevents the animal from having to exert itself unnecessarily fleeing from you.
- **Take only photographs.** Leave all natural things, features, and historic artifacts as you found them for others to enjoy.

- **Never roll rocks off trails or cliffs.** Gravity increases the impact of falling rocks exponentially, and you risk endangering lives below you.

HUNTING

Some of the destinations in this book (such as Green Mountain) are open to hunting. Season dates vary, but generally in Washington big-game hunting begins in early August and ends in late November. Some areas may also be open to bird hunting which generally takes place from Fall to mid-winter. While using trails in areas frequented by hunters, it is best to make yourself visible by donning an orange cap and vest. If hiking with a dog, your buddy should wear an orange vest too.

BEARS AND COUGARS

Washington harbors healthy populations of black bears, found in many of the parks and preserves along the urban fringe. If you encounter a bear while hiking, you usually just catch a glimpse of its bear behind. But occasionally the bruin may actually want to get a look at *you*.

To avoid an un-*bear*-able encounter, practice bear-aware prudence: Always keep a safe distance. Remain calm, do not look a bear in the eyes, speak in a low tone, and do not run from it. Hold your arms out to appear as big as possible. Slowly move away. The bear may bluff-charge—do not run. If it does charge, lie down and play dead, protecting your head and neck. Usually the bear will leave once he perceives he is not threatened. If he does attack, fight back using fists, rocks, trekking poles, or bear spray if you are carrying it.

Our state also supports a healthy population of *Felix concolor*. While cougar encounters are extremely rare, they do occur and occasionally in parks and preserves on the urban fringe. Cougars are cats—they're curious. They may follow hikers, but rarely (almost never) attack adult humans. Minimize contact by not hiking or running alone and avoiding

Point No Point Park offers fine beach walking in addition to trails.

carrion. If you do encounter a cougar, remember the big cat is looking for prey that can't, or won't fight back. Do not run, as this may trigger its prey instinct. Stand up and face it. If you appear aggressive, the cougar will probably back down. Wave your arms, trekking poles, or a jacket over your head to appear bigger and maintain eye contact. Pick up children and small dogs, and back away slowly if you can do so safely, not taking your eyes off of it. If the cougar attacks, throw things at it. Shout loudly. If it gets close, whack it with your trekking pole, if you have one, fighting back aggressively.

WATER AND GEAR

While most of the trails in this book can be enjoyed without much preparation or gear, it is always a good idea to bring water, even if you're just out for a quick walk or run. Even better, carry a small pack with water, a few snacks, sunglasses, and a rain jacket.

THE TEN ESSENTIALS

If you are heading out for a longer adventure—perhaps linking together several trails described here—consider packing

The Ten Essentials, items that are good to have on hand in an emergency:

- **Navigation.** Carry a map of the area you plan to be in and know how to read it. A cellphone and/or GPS unit are good to have along too.
- **Sun protection.** Even on wet days, carry sunscreen and sunglasses; you never know when the clouds will lift, and you can easily sunburn near water.
- **Insulation.** Storms can and do blow in rapidly. Carry raingear, wind gear, and extra layers.
- **Illumination.** If caught out after dark, you'll be glad you have a headlamp or flashlight so you can follow the trail home.
- **First-aid supplies.** At the very least, your kit should include: bandages, gauze, scissors, tape, tweezers, pain relievers, antiseptics, and perhaps a small manual.
- **Fire.** While being forced to spend the night out is not likely on these trails, a campfire could provide welcome warmth in an emergency, with matches kept dry in a zip-lock bag.
- **Repair kit and tools.** A pocketknife or multitool can come in handy, as can basic repair items such as nylon cord, safety pins, a small roll of duct tape, and a small tube of superglue.
- **Nutrition.** Pack a handful of nuts or sports bars for emergency pick-me-ups.
- **Hydration.** Bring enough water to keep you hydrated, and for longer treks consider a means of water purification.
- **Emergency shelter.** This can be as simple as a garbage bag, or a rain poncho that can double as an emergency tarp.

TRAILHEAD CONCERNS

By and large, our parks and trails are safe places. Common sense and vigilance, however, are still in order. This is true for all trail users, but particularly so for solo ones. Be aware of your surroundings at all times. Let someone know when and where you're headed out.

Car break-ins are a common occurrence at some of our parks and trailheads. Do not leave anything of value in your vehicle while out on the trail. Take your wallet, cellphone, and any listening devices with you. A duffel bag on the back seat may contain dirty T-shirts, but a thief may think there's a laptop in it.

If you arrive at a trailhead and someone looks suspicious, don't discount your intuition. If something doesn't feel right, it probably isn't. Take action by leaving the place or situation promptly. If the person behaves inappropriately or aggressively, take notes on their appearance, their vehicle's make and license plate, and report their behavior to the authorities. Do not confront the person; leave and go to another trail.

No need to be paranoid; the trails and parks are far safer here than in most urban areas. Just use a little common sense and vigilance while you're out and about.

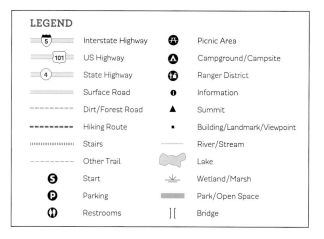

LEGEND

Interstate Highway	Picnic Area
US Highway	Campground/Campsite
State Highway	Ranger District
Surface Road	Information
Dirt/Forest Road	Summit
Hiking Route	Building/Landmark/Viewpoint
Stairs	River/Stream
Other Trail	Lake
Start	Wetland/Marsh
Parking	Park/Open Space
Restrooms	Bridge

Next page: Rocky Creek Conservation Area

KEY
PENINSULA

Named for its shape, the Key Peninsula (a sub-peninsula of the Kitsap) extends south from the Kitsap Peninsula for approximately 16 miles. Its name became official in 1980 when the Washington Board on Geographic Names formally accepted it. Prior to that, it was known as the Lower Kitsap or Longbranch Peninsula. Locals often refer to the peninsula as the Key or KP. Along with nearby Gig Harbor, the Key Peninsula is in Pierce County and has its own park district separate from Pierce and Kitsap counties. In recent years there has been a push by residents and government officials to expand the area's public lands and trails.

1   360 Trails

DISTANCE:	More than 8 miles of trails
ELEVATION GAIN:	Up to 250 feet
HIGH POINT:	325 feet
DIFFICULTY:	Easy to moderate
FITNESS:	Walkers, runners
FAMILY-FRIENDLY:	Heavy mountain bike use; use caution with young children on the park's singletrack trails
DOG-FRIENDLY:	On leash, and be aware of mountain bikers and equestrians on some trails
AMENITIES:	Picnic tables
CONTACT/MAP:	KeyPenParks, www.keypenparks.com/360-trails.html
GPS:	N47 23.353 W122 41.020
BEFORE YOU GO:	The park periodically closes for mountain bike events. Check the park website for closures.

GETTING THERE

Driving: From Bremerton, head south on State Route 16 to SR 302 in Purdy. (From Gig Harbor, head north on SR 16 to SR 302 in Purdy.) From the traffic light in Purdy, continue west on SR 302 for 3.3 miles, bearing right onto 144th Street NW (signed "Key Peninsula Parks 360 Trails"). Proceed 0.4 mile to the trailhead. Parking is at the trailhead.

While also open to horses and hikers, this fairly new park is especially popular with mountain bikers. A few of the trails were even built by and made specifically for mountain bikers and are closed to pedestrians. But the park's main loop (an old logging road) and several side trails make for satisfying walking and running routes in which to pound out a little mileage.

It's best to visit during the week, when the sprocket brigade is light. Although this former DNR property was logged not long ago, some groves of tall trees still stand, a pretty brook

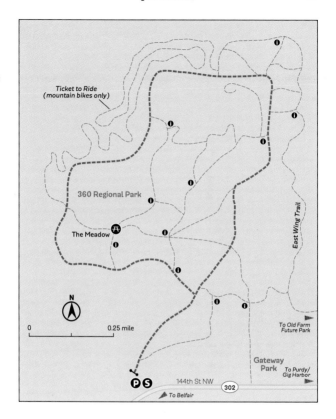

flows through the property, and deer and other critters make their home here.

GET MOVING

From the parking lot, follow a gated old road north. From this wide main trail, many user-built trails take off left and right. Several of the junctions are marked with posts and trail maps. The Main Trail gently climbs, coming to a major junction at 0.3 mile. Here you can make a loop of a little more than 2 miles by following the Main Trail, which rolls (gaining about 200

A thinned stand of stately second-growth Douglas fir

feet in cumulative elevation gain) through old selective cuts, groves of tall second-growth Douglas fir, and cleared areas being taken over by invasive Scotch broom.

Several singletrack trails of 0.1 to 0.5 mile in length lead left from the main trail and offer some nice loop options in generally forested areas. Several of the trails lead to an area known as The Meadow, a small grassy area with picnic tables surrounded by some tall firs. It's a nice place for a lunch break or gathering for a group run or walk.

Two trail networks take off right from the loop. The one to the northwest, Ticket to Ride, is for mountain bikers only. The East Wing is primarily a mountain biker trail, but hikers are welcome. This 1-mile trail drops into a ravine with a small creek, passing among some of the tallest and oldest trees in the park. From the East Wing, two trails branch south—one leading to Gateway Park (currently being developed with play fields), the other to an old farm, part of a 400-acre tract that Key Pen Parks purchased in 2012 and will be developing into a park with trails. Once completed, it'll be a great hiking and running destination.

2 Rocky Creek Conservation Area

DISTANCE:	More than 3 miles of trails
ELEVATION GAIN:	Up to 250 feet
HIGH POINT:	325 feet
DIFFICULTY:	Easy to moderate
FITNESS:	Hikers, runners
FAMILY-FRIENDLY:	Lightly traveled trails for children of all ages
DOG-FRIENDLY:	On leash
AMENITIES:	Benches
CONTACT/MAP:	Key Pen Parks, www.keypenparks.com/rocky-creek -conservation-area.html
GPS:	N47 23.134 W122 44.547

GETTING THERE

Driving: From Bremerton, head south on State Route 16 to SR 302 in Purdy. (From Gig Harbor, head north on SR 16 to SR 302 in Purdy.) From the traffic light in Purdy, continue west on SR 302 for 6.3 miles. Turn right onto 150th Avenue N and in 0.1 mile turn left onto Crews Road, which becomes the Elgin Clifton Access Road. Proceed for 0.5 mile to the trailhead on your left. Parking is at the trailhead.

Despite its proximity to State Route 302, the Rocky Creek Conservation Area is little known, little hiked, and in a more natural state than the popular 360 Park a few miles east (Hike 1). Here

Rocky Creek is a great place for spring woodland wildflowers.

you can wander along trails circling a large wetland in the heart of this 224-acre conservation area, and explore quiet side trails that lead to the small babbling creek for which this area is named.

GET MOVING

By combining the park's several trails which total more than 3 miles (shown on the trailhead kiosk map), you could easily spend a couple of hours here. While the trails are not well marked, you needn't worry about getting lost, as the park isn't very large and it's bordered on three sides by roads, including the Elgin Clifton

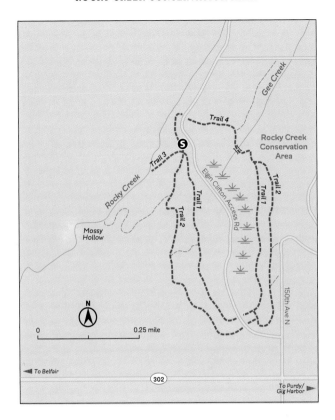

Access Road, which bisects the park and several of the trails. This road sees little traffic and can be safely walked as well.

Four trails depart from the trailhead, all marked with a start and finish post. Trail 3, the shortest, leaves directly west. Follow this nice wide trail through hemlocks and maples on a slight descent, reaching a bench at the shore of Rocky Creek at 0.15 mile.

Trails 1 and 2 leave south from the trailhead, running parallel around the large wetland in the center of the conservation area. They meet in the northeastern corner of the park with Trail 4, which leads back to the trailhead. The outer loop, Trails 2 and 4, is about 1.3 miles; the inner loop, Trails 1 and 4, is approximately 1.2 miles. Both routes traverse dry Douglas fir forest, climbing a small ridge heading south, then crossing the Elgin Clifton Access Road and climbing a small ridge north. The wetland is visible through the trees, but the best views are from along the road.

Where Trails 1 and 2 meet at the northeast end of the loops, continue on Trail 4, making a bridged crossing of Gee Creek in a small gulch, then climbing out of the creek gully to a junction. The trail right leads 0.2 mile to a powerline road that connects with the Elgin Clifton Access Road. Trail 4 continues left, soon crossing the Elgin Clifton Access Road; it then makes a little dip before climbing back to the trailhead in 0.25 mile.

About 0.15 mile from the trailhead kiosk, a short side trail off Trail 2 veers right into a thick understory of boxwood, descending about 80 feet to a quiet spot on Rocky Creek in 0.25 mile. Kids will enjoy this mossy little hollow.

(In the eastern end of the conservation area, two other short trails veer off Trail 2 leading to the Lake Holiday Housing Association development.)

3 Maple Hollow Park

DISTANCE:	1 mile round-trip
ELEVATION GAIN:	225 feet
HIGH POINT:	175 feet
DIFFICULTY:	Moderate
FITNESS:	Hikers
FAMILY-FRIENDLY:	The trail to the beach includes a steep section that may be challenging to young children
DOG-FRIENDLY:	On leash

Secluded beach at Maple Hollow Park

AMENITIES:	Privy, picnic tables
CONTACT/MAP:	Key Pen Parks, www.keypenparks.com/maple-hollow -park.html
GPS:	N47 17.855 W122 45.059

GETTING THERE

Driving: From Bremerton, head south on State Route 16 to SR 302 in Purdy. (From Gig Harbor, head north on SR 16 to SR 302 in Purdy.) From the traffic light in Purdy, continue west on SR 302 for 5.2 miles, bearing left at the light. Continue south on Key Peninsula Highway for 5.6 miles, turning left (0.5 mile south of the middle school) onto Van Beek Road. Drive

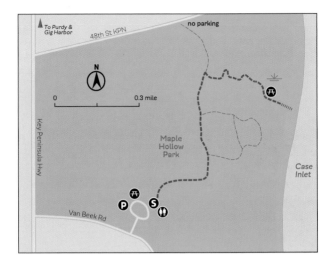

0.5 mile, then turn left into Maple Hollow Park. If the gate is closed, park at the gate and walk 0.1 mile to the trailhead.

A former DNR tract recently transferred to a park agency, Maple Hollow is far more valuable as parkland than as timberland, as protected shoreline on increasingly populated Puget Sound is in short supply. Visit this 58-acre park and discover the natural beauty of our grand inland waterway. Hike into a lush, dark ravine past huge monstrous maples and towering firs to emerge upon a beautiful, secluded beach on Case Inlet. Then saunter along the stone-strewn shore, savoring views of islands and peaks. On a warm sunny day, linger and cast your concerns to the Sound.

GET MOVING
From the parking area, follow a wide trail (ADA-accessible) 0.1 mile to a couple of old (from DNR days) interpretive panels. (Ignore the map on the panels, as the trail system has changed.) Then on a narrower path lined with evergreen huckleberry, begin

descending into a lush ravine shaded by impressive maples (hence Maple Hollow), firs, and cedars, soon reaching a junction.

The direct way to the beach leads straight. Or, turn right for a 0.25-mile loop above the forested beach bluff, and a glimpse of the inlet. The main trail soon intersects with the other end of the loop.

As you continue left on the main trail, now an old logging road, notice the change in the forest. This section of this small tract was logged in 1987, so the forest here is fairly young. Fortunately the old giants at the beginning of the hike were spared.

Climb 50 feet, and at 0.3 mile come to another junction. The trail left leads to 48th Street KPN (no parking); go right. Descending into a wetland area, you'll come to a picnic table and then a set of stairs leading down to the beach at 0.5 mile.

If the tide is low, you can wander on the public beach north for 0.1 mile and south for 0.15 mile. Admire the view to Fox and McNeil islands and Mount Rainier hovering to the south. Look north too, up Henderson Bay. Enjoy the peace of this off-the-beaten-path park, saving some energy for the climb back to your vehicle.

4 Penrose Point State Park

DISTANCE:	2.5 miles of trails
ELEVATION GAIN:	200 feet
HIGH POINT:	125 feet
DIFFICULTY:	Easy
FITNESS:	Walkers, hikers
FAMILY-FRIENDLY:	Wide, well-groomed trails, 2 miles of coastline, and forested campground make this park a family favorite
DOG-FRIENDLY:	On leash
AMENITIES:	Privies, water, benches, picnic tables, interpretive displays, campground

CONTACT/MAP:	Penrose Point State Park, (253) 884-2514,
	http://parks.state.wa.us/564/Penrose-Point
GPS:	N47 15.496 W122 44.730
BEFORE YOU GO:	Discover Pass required

GETTING THERE

Driving: From Bremerton, head south on State Route 16 to SR 302 in Purdy. (From Gig Harbor, head north on SR 16 to SR 302 in Purdy.) From the traffic light in Purdy, continue west on SR 302 for 5.2 miles, bearing left at the light. Drive 9 miles on Key Peninsula Highway, turning left onto Cornwall Road. In 0.4 mile turn right onto Delano Road and continue 0.9 mile to a four-way intersection. Turn left onto 158th Avenue and enter Penrose Point State Park, coming to a T junction at 0.5 mile. Bear right and continue 0.2 mile to the day-use parking area and trailhead.

Most visitors come to this old-estate-turned-park for its lovely beaches, campsites, and grassy shore-abutting picnic grounds. One of the prettiest state parks on Puget Sound, Penrose Point also offers more than 2 miles of hiking trails winding through the park's 160 acres. Hike through mature woods, along a quiet cove, and around the point to a beautiful bay, taking in sublime views of Mount Rainier rising over Puget Sound.

GET MOVING

On the south side of the day-use parking area, a trailhead kiosk marks the start of the park's main trail system. From here you can make a nearly 2-mile loop to Penrose Point and back, or a shorter loop using one of the connector trails. Junctions are signed with letters and often posted with a trail map as well.

For a scenic 1.9-mile coastal loop, hike left from junction A up an old roadway (you'll return via the trail on your right). Through a forest of big maples and alders, the trail rises to a

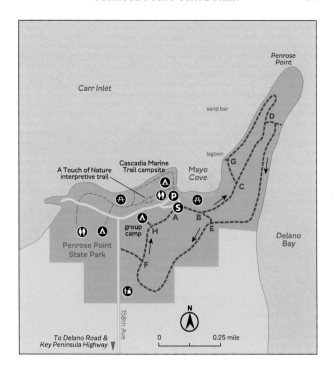

bluff above Mayo Cove. Go left at junction B, cross a creek, and in a 0.3 mile arrive at junction C. Turn left here for a trip around Penrose Point. Amble under a canopy of massive Douglas firs and madronas with flaky, rusted-looking bark. Coastal views are limited, but at junction G a short spur leads left to the shore. When the tide is low, you can walk along a spit protecting a lagoon and a sandbar extending into the cove.

The loop continues right through thick evergreen huckleberry "hedgerows" and a forest of mature madronas and firs. At 0.8 mile, come to junction D. The right fork leads back to the trailhead. Head left, and you'll soon come to beach access on Delano Bay. Check out the view from the beach,

Mount Rainier provides a scenic backdrop to Delano Bay

with Mount Rainier staring right at you from across the bay. Framing the bay are Fox Island to the southeast and Anderson Island to the southwest.

Continue hiking south along Delano Bay, enjoying the splendid views of Rainier. The trail eventually leaves the shoreline, climbing a small hillside forested with hardwoods. At 1.3 miles you arrive at junction E; here you can cut your loop short and return right to the trailhead. To complete the loop, turn left, climbing over a quiet knoll (elevation 120 feet). Just past a water tower, the trail starts to descend. Stay right at junction F where a trail leads left to the campground. Hike through a grove of big maples, skirting a group campsite, and stay right at junction H, returning to junction A to close the loop.

GO FARTHER

You can easily spend all day at Penrose Point. Heck, all night too—the park's campground invites an overnight stay. Additional hiking options include the 0.2-mile A Touch of Nature interpretive trail and a 0.5-trail to picnic areas along Mayo Cove. At low tide look for Native American petroglyphs on an exposed spit in the inner cove. You can also hike around Penrose Point on the beach at low tide. Mud and rocks can make it slow going, but it's worth the opportunity to see contorted bluffs shaped by the tides and winter storms.

Next page: Bridge over Gold Creek, Green Mountain State Forest

KITSAP PENINSULA

Jutting into Puget Sound like a big arrowhead, the Kitsap Peninsula is Washington's second great peninsula. With over 240 miles of coastline, and attached to the mainland by an isthmus less than 2 miles wide, Kitsap can feel like an island. But despite its geographical isolation, its proximity to Seattle and Tacoma via ferries and bridge has led to its development. Out of the state's thirty-nine counties, Kitsap ranks thirty-sixth in size but is the third most densely populated, with nearly 640 people per square mile (only King and Clark counties are more densely populated).

While development continues to transform large sections of the peninsula's rural charm into suburbia, large expanses remain fairly wild. Along Hood Canal on the peninsula's western shoreline, large tracts of forest and coastline remain undeveloped. But it won't stay this way without citizen involvement calling for conservation measures. The Great Peninsula Conservancy, a land trust in the county, has been instrumental in protecting thousands of acres of key shoreline and forest lands. The Kitsap County Parks Department has also accelerated its land acquisitions within the past decade. This has all led to a huge increase in public lands and trails, making Kitsap County a Puget Sound hotspot for hiking and trail running. The land trust and parks department continue to work on easements and purchases with many new and exciting projects in the works. Stay tuned.

Kitsap takes its name from Chief Kitsap of the Suquamish Tribe. It was originally named Slaughter County after Lieutenant William A. Slaughter of the US Army who perished in the Indian War of 1855–56, but that name was short-lived. Kitsap means "brave and good," hence the local land trust's name for it, the Great Peninsula.

5 McCormick Forest

DISTANCE:	4 miles of trail
ELEVATION GAIN:	Up to 150 feet
HIGH POINT:	325 feet
DIFFICULTY:	Easy to moderate
FITNESS:	Hikers, runners
FAMILY-FRIENDLY:	The wooded trails are great for young children; be aware of some steep spots near the creek, and that some trails are open to horses
DOG-FRIENDLY:	On leash; be aware of mountain bikers and equestrians on some trails
AMENITIES:	Privy, doggie-bag dispensers, picnic tables
CONTACT/MAP:	PenMet Parks, www.penmetparks.org/parks-trails/parks/mccormick-forest-park
GPS:	N47 21.134 W 122 37.269

GETTING THERE

Driving: From Bremerton, head south on State Route 16 to the Burnham Drive exit and west through the roundabout to Sehmel Drive. (From Tacoma, head north on SR 16 to the Burnham Drive exit and head west at the roundabout , crossing over the highway, and continue west through the second roundabout to Sehmel Drive.) Turn left on Sehmel Drive and continue for 0.5 mile. Turn left onto Bujacich Road, with parking for McCormick Forest immediately on your left. Additional parking can be found across Bujacich Road at the Fire District 5 headquarters.

Transit: Pierce Transit Route 100 Gig Harbor stops at Borgen Boulevard and 51st Avenue NW; from there walk 0.8 mile to the park.

Long known among area runners as the Jail Woods for its proximity to the Washington Corrections Center for Women, this 122-acre forested parcel is now a PenMet Park with a

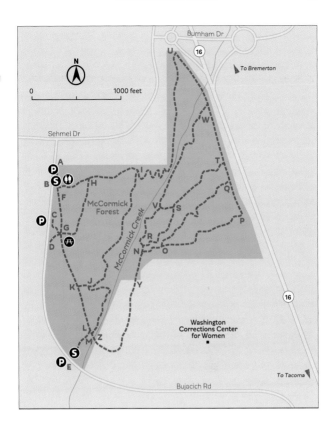

well-marked and -maintained trail system. A favorite area for local runners, it also should satisfy hikers and walkers out for reflective nature outings.

GET MOVING
While small, this park is crisscrossed with trails, so be sure to download a map and take it along until you learn the trail system. Twenty-five junctions are marked with lettered posts, A through Z (with no X marking the spot), and in some locations

A stately Douglas fir at McCormick Forest

a map. Posts also name local businesses that have adopted a section of trail to maintain.

Much of McCormick Forest is comprised of mature second-growth fir and hemlock with a thick understory of salal and evergreen huckleberry. Some sections of huckleberry are so thick, it's like hiking in a corn maze. There are small steep sections along the park's western and northern boundaries and gentler terrain along its east and south. The most interesting feature of the park is McCormick Creek, flowing through a small ravine. The ravine is graced with some big old cedars and firs and thick boughs of ferns giving it a wild feeling—even though the buzz of SR 16 can be heard in the background. Trails travel along and through the ravine.

You could spend a couple of hours exploring the ravine and forest through a myriad of trail combinations. Challenge yourself by trying to do all (or as many) of the trails as you can without repeating a section. While the park's trails are well marked, the distances aren't. Most junctions are just a tenth of a mile apart. A walk along the park's periphery, which includes a couple of small climbs and two creek crossings, makes a nice 2-mile loop. The trail from junction R to junction W into the ravine and along the creek is just shy of a half mile, and is probably the prettiest section in the park, traversing attractive old-growth forest.

GO FARTHER

If you're looking to ramp up the mileage, walk across Bujacich Road to the trails of the 97-acre Rotary Bark Park (see Hike 6), combining the two parks for a longer workout.

6   Rotary Bark Park

DISTANCE:	3 miles of trails
ELEVATION GAIN:	Up to 150 feet
HIGH POINT:	350 feet
DIFFICULTY:	Easy to moderate
FITNESS:	Walkers, hikers, runners
FAMILY-FRIENDLY:	Kid-friendly, but watch for runners on some of the curving trails
DOG-FRIENDLY:	The park includes a large enclosed off-leash dog park with trails; other trails are dog-friendly and require a leash
AMENITIES:	Privy, doggie-bag dispensers, picnic tables
CONTACT/MAP:	PenMet Parks, www.penmetparks.org/parks-trails /parks/rotary-bark-park

GPS: N47 21.063 W122 37.317

BEFORE YOU GO: The park is open from 7:00 AM to dusk. Dogs must be leashed outside of the off-leash area; the trails are open to horses. While you may notice jugs of water at the entrance of the off-leash area, don't rely on them for your pooch; be sure to pack your own water supply.

GETTING THERE

Driving: From Bremerton, head south on State Route 16 to the Burnham Drive exit and west through the roundabout to Sehmel Drive. (From Tacoma, head north on SR 16 to the Burnham Drive exit and head west at the roundabout crossing over the highway, and continue west through the second roundabout to Sehmel Drive.) Turn left on Sehmel Drive and continue for 0.5 mile. Turn left onto Bujacich Road, where parking for the park can be found immediately on your right at the Gig Harbor Fire & Medic One Fire District #5 Headquarters.

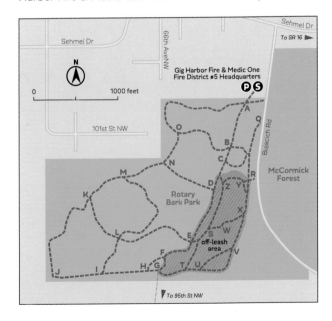

Happy four-legged hikers and their humans at the Rotary Bark Park

Transit: Pierce Transit Route 100 Gig Harbor stops at Borgen Boulevard and 51st Avenue NW; from there walk 0.8 mile to the park.

Many dog parks consist of a small gated area enclosing a muddy romping ground, but not this one. Rotary Bark Park's main draw is its 15-acre wooded off-leash area traversed by trails, but with or without a pooch, you'll want to explore the rest of its 97 acres. More than 3 miles of interconnecting trails traverse this forested and hilly park, a favorite of local trail runners. It's just across Bujacich Road from the 122-acre McCormick Forest (Hike 5), so many hikers and runners combine these two parks for long workouts and adventures.

This exceptional park came to be through a partnership with the Peninsula School District, Gig Harbor Fire & Medic One, PenMet Parks, and the local Rotary Club. As with most of our parks, volunteers, nonprofit organizations, and business partnerships have been integral to its establishment, upkeep, and protection.

GET MOVING

From the trailhead you can follow a procession of diverse doggies and their humans heading south on a wide path. Be sure your pup is leashed until you get to the gate. You'll soon come to junction A, the first of twenty-six junctions marked by lettered posts (P being the parking lot).

After a pleasant 0.3-mile walk to the gated off-leash area, enter and let Rover run free. (Runners, however, are not free to run here; keep that activity outside of the dog park.) A wide 0.5-mile trail circles the periphery of the off-leash area, traversed by connecting trails.

From junction A you can follow the main trail to the dog park, then south another 0.3 mile to junction G (where a short path leads out of the park to 95th Street NW; no parking). From there you can head right (west) and follow the trail along the periphery of the park, returning to the parking lot in 1.8 miles. This loop includes a drop and climb of 150 vertical feet. Most of the way is through mature second-growth Douglas fir with an understory of evergreen huckleberry. At the periphery's low point, you'll cross a little creek on a small bridge. Trails branch off from the periphery paths toward the park's interior, allowing for lots of loop options.

7 Sehmel Homestead Park

DISTANCE:	4 miles of trails
ELEVATION GAIN:	Up to 100 feet
HIGH POINT:	125 feet
DIFFICULTY:	Easy

Pastoral meadow at Sehmel Homestead Park

FITNESS:	Walkers, hikers, runners
FAMILY-FRIENDLY:	The wide Sehmel Perimeter Loop is jogger-stroller friendly; other trails are good for young children. Some trails are open to bikes and horses, so be aware.
DOG-FRIENDLY:	On leash, and be aware of bikers and equestrians
AMENITIES:	Privy, drinking water, doggie-bag dispensers, picnic tables; pavilion, amphitheater, meeting rooms, and party room available for rentals
CONTACT/MAP:	PenMet Parks, www.penmetparks.org/parks-trails /parks/sehmel-homestead-park#description
GPS:	N47 21.043 W122 38.486

GETTING THERE

Driving: From Bremerton, head south on State Route 16 to the Burnham Drive exit and head west at the roundabout to Sehmel Drive. (From Tacoma, head north on SR 16 to the Burnham Drive exit and head west at the roundabout; cross over the highway, and continue west through the second roundabout to Sehmel Drive.) Turn left on Sehmel Drive and continue for 1.6 miles. Then turn left onto 78th Avenue NW, proceeding 0.2 mile to the park entrance.

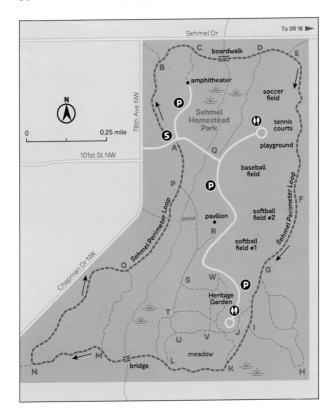

The Sehmel Homestead Park is not only one of PenMet's newest parks, but also one of the agency's finest, with well-groomed trails (including some open to bikes and horses), sport fields, gardens, and attractive structures available for rent. Some of the original fields and orchards remain from the 1880s homestead, helping to showcase the area's heritage.

This 98-acre park was once part of a much larger tract first homesteaded in the 1880s by Henry Sehmel, an immigrant from Germany. He was eventually joined by his two brothers, working more than 500 contiguous acres. In 2002

Pierce County Parks and Recreation purchased this 98-acre parcel from his descendants, for a multiuse park. While the playfields are the most active part of the park, 76 acres of the Sehmel Homestead are in a natural state, offering 4 miles of trails for walkers, hikers, and runners.

GET MOVING

The most popular trail is the wide and well-groomed 1.9-mile Sehmel Perimeter Loop, which skirts the park's ballfields and natural areas and connects to a series of secondary paths. You can access the perimeter trail from several points, including junction A, just south of the large parking lot near the amphitheater (used for performing arts) near the park's entrance. As in other nearby PenMet parks, junctions are marked by lettered posts.

Follow the perimeter trail clockwise through the alphabet, first through a rolling field lined with maples, then reaching a wide boardwalk over a wetland. The trail then skirts the ballfields and then thick woods where a singletrack loop diverges left into the forest. The perimeter trail traverses a pleasant meadow before dropping into a forested ravine cradling a small creek. Here at junction L a side trail heads north along the creek wetland, connecting back with the perimeter trail and to trails leading to the heritage garden.

The perimeter loop continues west, crossing the creek on a boardwalk and passing another trail paralleling the creek. The perimeter trail then heads up a small forested hill, bends north, and traverses another field before returning to the park access road. Make sure any young walkers with you look left to see a handful of cow silhouettes in the field.

GO FARTHER

You can easily double your mileage by hiking the wetland and forest trails in combination with the loop. Some paved walkways run along the park's access road and around one of the ballfields, ideal for wheelchairs and strollers. Walkers looking for a reflective stroll will enjoy the quiet paths weaving through the Heritage and Master Gardener demonstration gardens. Check the park's website for recreational camps and classes.

8 Cushman Powerline Trail

DISTANCE:	6.2 miles one-way
ELEVATION GAIN:	Up to 700 feet
HIGH POINT:	325 feet
DIFFICULTY:	Easy to moderate
FITNESS:	Walkers, runners
FAMILY-FRIENDLY:	Stroller-friendly and ADA-accessible, although the northern half includes several short steep hills; provides access to several abutting kid-friendly parks like Wilkinson Farm Park.
DOG-FRIENDLY:	On leash
AMENITIES:	Privies, benches
CONTACT/MAP:	PenMet Parks and City of Gig Harbor Parks, www.cityofgigharbor.net/cushman-trail
GPS:	Northern Trailhead N47 21.469 W122 36.572

GETTING THERE

Driving: There are four trailheads with parking, and the trail can be accessed from other points along the way. Find parking at mile 0 on 14th Avenue NW (0.3 mile north of the junction with 24th Street near the intersection with SR 16); near mile 3 at Pierce Transit Park and Ride on Kimball Drive and Grandview Forest Park on Grandview Street; and at mile 6.2 on Borgen Boulevard (0.1 mile west of the Burnham Drive roundabout near the SR 16 intersection). Parking is also available at Wilkinson Farm Park on Rosedale Street where a short trail will lead you to near mile 4 on the Cushman Powerline Trail.

Long boardwalk at the northern end of Cushman Powerline Trail

Transit: Pierce Transit Route 100 Gig Harbor stops at Park and Ride near mile 3 on Kimball Drive, and on Olympic Drive near mile 2 at Cushman Trailhead Park.

Bisecting the city of Gig Harbor from north to south, the Cushman Powerline Trail is easily accessible and always abuzz with walkers, runners, and bicyclists of all ages and abilities. Threading several smaller city parks, the trail offers park-to-park walking and running opportunities. It also skirts several eateries, allowing for good post-workout carbo-loading opportunities.

GET MOVING

With its recent extension all the way to Borgen Boulevard, the Cushman Powerline Trail now extends for 6.2 miles. That's 10 kilometers—a popular running race distance. Leave a vehicle at one end of the trail and start at the other, and train for this distance by doing the trail one-way. It makes for a perfect conditioning route too, with its long gentle inclines and declines and several short, steep sections.

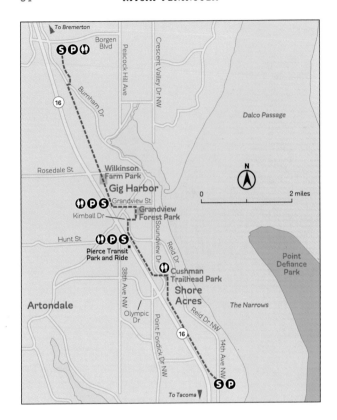

Primarily following a powerline right-of-way, this trail doesn't approach hills gently like a rail trail. Trail designers did put some curves in the long hilly sections, easing the grade somewhat, but expect to burn some calories where contours are crowded. The northern half of the trail is definitely hillier and more challenging than the southern half—but it is also more interesting, utilizing a much less developed corridor. We'll begin at the north trailhead on Borgen Boulevard.

Around mile 5.5 is a particularly interesting section of trail utilizing a graded boardwalk through a wetland swath. At mile 4, pass through the historic Wilkinson Farm where you can divert onto quiet trails through a holly grove and some pastures. South of the farm the trail passes over its highest hills, with limited views over Gig Harbor to Vashon Island and the Cascades.

Near mile 3 the trail passes city hall and Grandview Forest Park, with a few short side trails to explore. From here south, the trail traverses a more urban setting, including some sidewalks. This stretch appeals more to bike commuters and long-distance runners than to recreational walkers. The trail is marked at half-mile intervals, making it easy to keep track of your distance without having to carry a fancy GPS apparatus. Hills are signed too with grade warnings, some at 10 percent—that's steep. But, think of the great hill and interval training you can do on these big speed bumps!

GO FARTHER

At mile 0 on 14th Avenue NW, heading south, it is about 0.8 mile via 14th Avenue and 24th Street to the Scott Pierson Trail. This paved trail extends to Tacoma via the Tacoma Narrows Bridge, and the section over the bridge is a very popular running route for folks on both sides of the Narrows. The Stanich Trail along Gig Harbor's waterfront is actually a series of sidewalks and bike paths but is highly scenic, passing piers, businesses, and parks, offering lots of great sightseeing including views of Mount Rainier across the harbor. It makes for a great walk—and a good run when not crowded.

9 Anderson Point Trail

DISTANCE:	1.4 miles round-trip
ELEVATION GAIN:	250 feet
HIGH POINT:	250 feet
DIFFICULTY:	Moderate

FITNESS:	Walkers, hikers
FAMILY-FRIENDLY:	The beach is sandy and family-friendly; the access road/trail is steep and rocky in spots, making it difficult (but not impossible) to push a jogging stroller
DOG-FRIENDLY:	On leash
CONTACT/MAP:	Kitsap County Parks, www.kitsapgov.com/parks/Parks/Pages/regionalparks/anderson_point_county_park.htm
GPS:	N47 26.305 W122 32.383
BEFORE YOU GO:	The park is open from 6:00 AM to 8:30 PM; do not park along Millihanna Road (subject to ticketing and towing).

GETTING THERE

Driving: From State Route 16 in Port Orchard, follow SR 160 (Sedgwick Road) east for 5 miles. Turn right onto Banner Road and proceed south for 4.5 miles, turning left onto Millihanna Road. Continue 0.3 mile to Anderson Point County Park entrance and trailhead. Parking is at the trailhead.

From Gig Harbor, follow SR 16 north and exit onto Burley Olalla Road. Follow this road east for 2.4 miles, bearing right onto Olalla Valley Road. Continue east for 1.5 miles and turn left onto Banner Road. After 1.6 miles, turn right on Millihanna Road and continue for 0.3 mile to Anderson Point County Park entrance and trailhead. Parking is at the trailhead.

The Anderson Point trail leads to one of the finest strands of sandy beach on the Kitsap Peninsula; visit on a warm sunny day and linger long. Languidly stroll along 2000 feet of scenic shoreline, savoring sweeping views across Colvos Passage of Vashon Island. It's quite a drop reaching this sweet spot, so save some energy for the return hike.

This 66-acre Kitsap County Park recently reopened after a five-year closure due to a series of slides. Following negotiations among concerned parties, the access road was improved and the trailhead parking area expanded, restoring public access.

GET MOVING

Follow the trail (actually a gated dirt road) downward off a bluff into a lush ravine. The way is well shaded thanks to a thick green canopy of maples and alders. Cross some of the newly stabilized slide areas and get a sneak peek of the salt-water below.

At 0.7 mile reach the grassy flat of Anderson Point, and its expansive and gorgeous beach, nearly 2000 feet of frontage along Colvos Passage. As you walk the public beach, be sure to respect private property at either end. Find a nice spot to

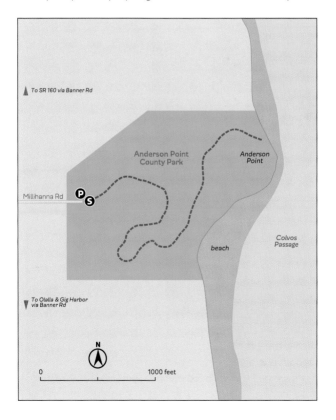

Wide sandy beach at Anderson Point

picnic, nap, and play. Across Colvos Passage admire the fairly undeveloped shoreline of Vashon Island. If it's a clear day, look north and see Mount Baker floating on the horizon.

10

Banner Forest Heritage Park

DISTANCE:	29 miles of trails
ELEVATION GAIN:	Up to several hundred feet
HIGH POINT:	430 feet
DIFFICULTY:	Easy to moderate
FITNESS:	Hikers, runners
FAMILY-FRIENDLY:	Most trails are suitable for young children, but best to avoid the most popular mountain biking routes; trails in the wetland easement zone are closed to bikes. The service road is bumpy but doable for jogging strollers.
DOG-FRIENDLY:	On leash; be aware of horse and bike use on many of the trails
CONTACT/MAP:	Kitsap County Parks, www.kitsapgov.com/parks/Parks/Pages/heritageparks/banner_forest.htm
GPS:	N47 29.355 W122 32.761

GETTING THERE

Driving: From State Route 16 in Port Orchard, follow SR 160 east for 4.8 miles, turning right onto Banner Road SE. (From Southworth Ferry, follow SR 160 west for 2.5 miles, turning left onto Banner Road SE.) Continue 1.1 miles to the trailhead on your right. Parking is at the trailhead.

Transit: Kitsap Transit #85 (Mullenix Express) will make a flagged stop.

While Banner Forest is a popular Kitsap trail-running and mountain-biking spot, casual hikers and dog-walkers will find it to their liking as well. Explore a spaghetti heap of trails that twist, turn, and tangle their way through mature second-growth forest. Explore wetland pools in the heart of the forest and amble aimlessly on paths sporting colorful names.

There are 29 miles of named trails traversing just about every hollow and grove in this 635-acre park, with several

CREATING GREAT PARKS AND TRAILS ON THE GREAT PENINSULA

Until not that long ago, hiking options were pretty limited on the Kitsap Peninsula. The peninsula's population, however, continues to grow, spurred by Navy personnel, retirees, urban refugees, and Seattle commuters looking for quieter and more affordable neighborhoods. Kitsap County's population alone is more than a quarter million—and a lot of those folks are hikers, runners, and walkers. Thankfully, in the past decade the peninsula's parks and trails have grown significantly to help accommodate the area's demand for outdoor recreation destinations. And you can thank a couple of active nonprofit land trusts and a coalition of trail advocates for making this happen. These groups are all worth joining and would love to have you on board helping them to continue expanding Kitsap's parks and trails.

The Great Peninsula Conservancy has been instrumental in helping protect nearly 6000 acres, including the Banner Forest and Clear Creek Trail corridor. The Bainbridge Island Land Trust has helped protect over 1300 acres of land, including the Grand Forest and Gazzam Lake. Forterra is a large conservation organization that is active throughout the Puget Sound area and beyond. They are currently involved with protecting the Grover's Creek Preserve, adjacent to the North Kitsap Heritage Park and the Port Gamble lands. They have also, along with the above land trusts, secured conservation easements on many other properties allowing private landowners to preserve, farm, or sustainably harvest timber on their lands without threat of development.

The Kitsap Forest & Bay Project is a community-wide consortium of business leaders and conservation groups intent on conserving nearly 7000 acres of forest and 1.8 miles of shoreline on the Kitsap Peninsula. The North Kitsap Trails Association formed to "unite North Kitsap County with a regional trail system of land and water trails." They have been instrumental in working with other groups securing the former Port Gamble timberlands, creating and maintaining trails on those lands, and in securing a corridor for the proposed Sound to Olympics Trail. They are also one of the groups involved with the Kitsap Forest & Bay Project. This coalition is a community-wide effort that includes state and local government agencies, local tribes, nonprofit groups, local businesses, and citizens, all working to conserve 7000 acres of the Port Gamble lands.

more miles of unnamed trails intertwined among those paths. None of them were officially built, and many were built specifically by and for mountain bikers, with sharp twists and sinuous routes. Kitsap County Parks acquired the Banner Forest in 2000 from the Washington State Department of Natural Resources after that agency was intent on swapping the parcel with a private developer. Today, instead of sporting hundreds of homes, this large open space is enjoyed by hundreds of hikers, bikers, and runners.

Kitsap County Parks has been working with user groups and committees on upgrading several of the trails, rerouting others, and closing a few (mainly the unnamed ones). Volunteers have been active in maintaining trails, signing them, and mapping the park.

The Great Peninsula Conservancy holds a conservation easement on 139 acres within the heart of the forest. This core section contains a wetland complex of ecological importance. Bikes are prohibited on the trails within the easement, allowing for better resource protection and quiet hiking options.

GET MOVING

Most trail junctions are marked, but you'll have a hard time not going astray hiking in the Banner Forest. Carry a map, but even then you may still be perplexed encountering Banner Forest's myriad of junctions and trails. Just about all of the trails lead back to the park's service road (known as the Access Road) or a main trail connecting with the service road, so don't worry about getting lost. Make going astray part of the adventure.

From the main parking lot, follow a well-beaten trail a short distance to the Access Road. Horseshoeing through the park, this gently rolling old woods road makes for a fine hike. It travels for 2.2 miles to terminate on the SE Olalla Valley Road where parking is also available. Hike the Access Road out and back, or consider combining it with some of the trails diverting from it, for a loop.

Many of the trails that branch off west of the Access Road mainly appeal to mountain bikers. For hikers and runners, the trails leading into the conservation-easement interior are better choices.

Make a loop by following the Access Road for 1.8 miles and returning via the 0.7-mile Banner Slough Trail (which can be muddy in wet weather) back to the Access Road where it is 0.3 mile to the trailhead.

A longer loop option is to hike the complete Access Road for 2.2 miles and return on the 0.9-mile Banner Alley Trail

The Banner Alley Trail cuts through thick forest.

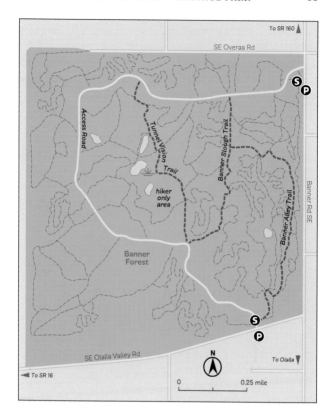

which leads to the Banner Slough Trail. Turn right and hike 0.2 mile to the Access Road, then head right 0.3 mile to the trailhead.

The Tunnel Vision Trail (reached by hiking the Access Road for 0.7 mile) is perhaps the most interesting trail in the park, bringing you to the core of the wetland conservation area. There's also an old moss-enveloped truck on this trail that children will find intriguing. This trail reconnects with the Access Road in 0.8 mile. From there you can return to the trailhead via the Banner Slough Trail or walk the Access Road

1.8 miles back. Other trails spoke off the Tunnel Vision Trail near the wetlands are also worth checking out. Most of them lead back to the Access Road. Have fun exploring and perhaps even getting temporarily lost.

11 Twanoh Creek Loop

DISTANCE:	2.3 miles round-trip
ELEVATION GAIN:	400 feet
HIGH POINT:	450 feet
DIFFICULTY:	Moderate
FITNESS:	Hikers, runners
FAMILY-FRIENDLY:	Wonderful trail for children, with big trees and a cascading creek
DOG-FRIENDLY:	On leash
AMENITIES:	Water, restrooms, picnic tables, campground (open year round)
CONTACT/MAP:	Twanoh State Park, (360) 275-2222, http://parks.state.wa.us/294/Twanoh
GPS:	N47 22.661 W122 58.395
BEFORE YOU GO:	A Discover Pass is required to enter the park.

GETTING THERE

Driving: From Bremerton, head west on State Route 3 to Belfair. Continue west on SR 106 for 7.8 miles to Twanoh State Park. Turn left into the campground entrance and park in the day-use parking area, before the camping information station.

Transit: Mason County Transit Route 2 will stop at the park if you request it.

Twanoh State Park protects 182 acres of mature forest, creek ravine, and beach on Hood Canal. The name Twanoh is derived from the Skokomish people, meaning "gathering place"—and this green refuge is a perfect place for people and wildlife to gather. The park contains 2.5 miles of trail,

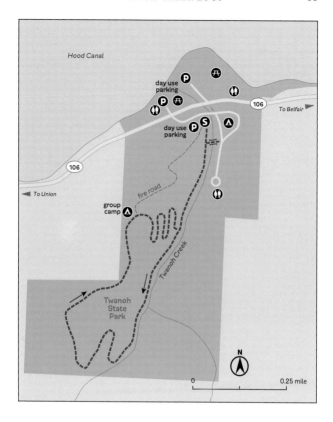

including this popular loop along a salmon spawning stream in a lush, emerald ravine.

GET MOVING

The wide and well-groomed trail begins on the south side of the campground entrance at the Twanoh Creek bridge, taking off through a cluster of rhododendrons. Heading upstream along gurgling Twanoh Creek, the trail skirts some choice creek-side campsites, soon reaching a junction where a bridge (popular with young campers) leads left to the campground.

Old-growth forest along Twanoh Creek

The trail continues straight through a verdant tunnel of rhododendrons and cedars up the small ravine with its bubbling waterway. The surrounding forest was logged over a century ago, leaving springboard-notched cedar stumps smothered in moss and engulfed by clumps of ferns. A few big trees remain, however.

At 0.3 mile you'll reach a junction for the loop. Most folks do the loop clockwise, preferring a steadier ascent over a steeper one. Following the trail in this fashion, continue along the creek a short way before beginning to climb out of the increasingly tight ravine. Vegetation along the forest floor changes to salal and evergreen huckleberry, indicating a drier climate above the ravine. After two switchbacks, the trail crests the top of the ravine, reaching an old woods road (elev. 450 feet) at 1.3 miles.

The loop now utilizes the old road, heading right and slowly descending. At 1.8 miles it passes through a group campsite. Shortly beyond is another junction. The fire road continues straight, leading back to the day-use parking area and can be used as an alternative return. The loop continues right, switchbacking down into the ravine. Passing beneath a few big old Douglas firs and clusters of leathery-leaved rhododendrons, the trail returns to the loop junction at 2 miles. From here it's 0.3 mile left back to the trailhead.

GO FARTHER

After your hike, carefully cross State Route 106 to the day-use area and follow Twanoh Creek to its small delta on Hood Canal. Walk along the beach or go for a swim in some of the warmest saltwater in the state. Check out the many Civilian Conservation Corp–built structures in the park, and the interpretive displays. And consider pitching your tent for a night in Twanoh's shaded creekside campground.

12 Theler Wetlands

DISTANCE:	3 miles of trails
ELEVATION GAIN:	40 feet
HIGH POINT:	40 feet
DIFFICULTY:	Easy
FITNESS:	Walkers, hikers
FAMILY-FRIENDLY:	Exceptional kid-friendly hiking area with boardwalks, outdoor exhibits, and wildlife viewing; trails ADA-accessible
DOG-FRIENDLY:	Dogs prohibited
AMENITIES:	Privies, benches, observation decks, outdoor education center

CONTACT/MAP:	Theler Community Center and Wetland Trails, www.thelertrails.org
GPS:	N 47 26.286 W 122 50.194
BEFORE YOU GO:	The preserve is open from dawn to dusk.

GETTING THERE

Driving: From Bremerton, head west on State Route 3 to Belfair, proceeding 1 mile past the junction with SR 300 to the Mary E. Theler Community Center (sign for nature trail), located on your right. (From Shelton, the community center is located on SR 3 0.5 mile north of the junction with SR 106.) Park at the community center.

Transit: The Theler Center is serviced by Mason County Transit Route 1 and 2 from Shelton; Route 3 from Bremerton; and Route 4 in Belfair.

Spend a couple of hours or all day exploring a wildlife-rich estuary at the farthest reaches of fjord-like Hood Canal. Watch for eagles, osprey, herons, swallows, otters, and deer as you hike the trails and boardwalks through grassy wetlands and along the Union River.

Among the many legacies that Sam and Mary Theler left to the town of Belfair was land for a Masonic lodge, church, and school. Of the 70 acres left to the North Mason School District arose the Mary E. Theler Wetlands Nature Preserve. Serving an educational role for area schoolchildren, the wetlands are open to folks of all ages and make for an excellent introduction to estuary ecology. The preserve has since been expanded to 139 acres and contains five distinct trails. Washington Department of Fish and Wildlife (WDFW) own several hundred acres of abutting land helping to protect this important ecosystem.

GET MOVING

Begin your hike on the Rock Wall Trail, passing under the welcome arch and proceeding 0.25 mile to the Wetlands Project

Family-friendly hiking at Theler Wetlands

Center. Whatever your age, the displays and hands-on exhibits will give you a better appreciation and understanding of the complex ecosystem you are about to explore. The gray whale skeleton will certainly pique some interest. Mosey around the native plant demonstration garden too—a great way to learn some of the many plants growing in the region. There are lots of artistic displays too to admire.

Several trails radiate from the nature center, allowing for out-and-back excursions and a few loops as well. The 0.1-mile Sweetwater Creek Trail loops from the center to the creek, passing several interpretive displays.

The 0.25-mile South Tidal Marsh Trail takes you over a long boardwalk to an observation deck at the edge of Hood Canal. Bird-watching from this post is excellent, including the flocks of swallows that nest along the boardwalk. You can view the southern Olympic mountain peaks from here as well.

The 0.3-mile Alder Creek Swamp loops back to the nature center after traversing wetlands on a boardwalk, a good vantage point for spotting birds among the grasses and reeds.

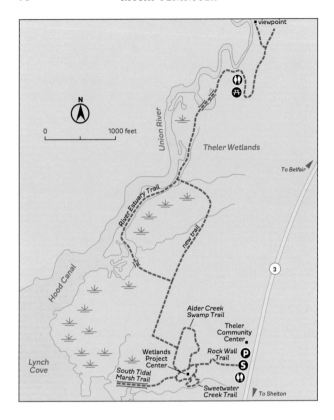

This trail ties into the River Estuary Trail, offering a much longer hike.

Leading northeast from the nature center, the 1.5-mile River Estuary Trail travels along an old dike across open wetlands, through a tunnel of shrubs and along active farmland, toward the mouth of the Union River. At the trail's second sharp turn it meets a new trail, which offers a loop option for return. (This trail leads east across WDFW property, eventually meeting up again with the River Estuary Trail in about a half mile.)

The main River Estuary Trail bends left (northwest) and soon comes to a long bridge, one of several new breaches allowing for restoration of parts of the delta that were diked and farmed in the past. Soon after the bridge, the trail reaches the Union River where it now follows this nutrient-rich waterway upstream.

After meeting the other end of the new trail, the River Estuary Trail crosses a set of bridges and reaches a small picnic area and restroom. At the terminus are two short spurs; the one left leads to a cedar grove at the river's edge for prime viewing of waterfowl and spawning salmon (in season).

Return to the Theler Wetlands at different times of the year to fully appreciate the life cycles at work in this ecologically important preserve.

13 Square Lake

DISTANCE:	1 mile round-trip
ELEVATION GAIN:	90 feet
HIGH POINT:	460 feet
DIFFICULTY:	Moderate
FITNESS:	Hikers
FAMILY-FRIENDLY:	The trail is brushy, not suitable for young children
DOG-FRIENDLY:	On leash
AMENITIES:	Privy, picnic tables
CONTACT/MAP:	Manchester State Park, (360) 871-4065, www.parks.wa.gov/542/Manchester (no map available)
GPS:	N47 28.813 W122 41.063
BEFORE YOU GO:	Square Lake State Park is open summer months from 8:00 AM to dusk; a Discover Pass is required.

GETTING THERE

Driving: From State Route 16 in Port Orchard (milepost 25), follow Sedgewick Road west for 0.8 mile. Bear left onto

Aquatic plants ring Square Lake.

Glenwood Road and proceed for 1.1 miles, bearing right onto SW Lake Flora Road. Continue 0.9 mile and turn right onto Square Lake Road SW. Follow this road 0.3 mile to the state park. Park in the lot at the end of the road.

Few folks know of this beautiful, little undeveloped lake just a few minutes from Port Orchard. Protected within a 237-acre state park and adjacent to a large county heritage park in the making, this greenbelt encompassing Square Lake currently has very little infrastructure in place. For now, take to some old woods roads for peaceful and lonely wandering.

Square Lake is one of a string of small lakes in rapidly developing southwestern Kitsap County. Local conservationists and government officials have recently been acquiring tracts of lands encompassing these lakes, important for wildlife habitat and providing excellent recreational opportunities.

While Kitsap County Parks has secured nearly 1200 acres for the Coulter Creek Heritage Park, there are currently no trails, parking, or facilities for visitors. Washington State Parks manages the adjacent 237-acre Square Lake and 118-acre Camp Calvinwood tracts. While the latter—an old church camp—currently can only be visited by reservation, Square Lake State Park with its picnic grounds and old woods roads is open for exploration.

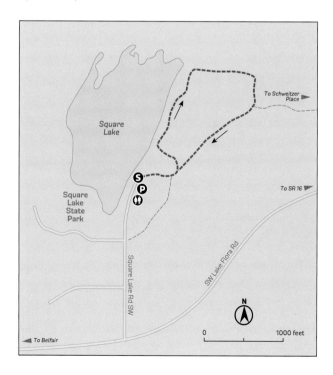

GET MOVING

From the parking lot, locate an old track heading east and uphill. Follow it into a young forest shading thick patches of salal and boxwood. After 0.1 mile reach a junction. Head left and descend toward the lake. Here you'll catch good glimpses of the actually round lake surrounded by a more-or-less square patch of bog. The lake teems with lilies and aquatic life. Birds are abundant too. And beavers—see their huts?

Now follow the old road north. It eventually pulls away from the lake and climbs back up a small ridge. After skirting a private residence, the trail comes to a junction at 0.5 mile. The way left leads downhill, petering out on Schweitzer Place. It's all within the park, but the way is overgrown. Instead head right for pleasant walking, eventually coming back to your first junction. Either head right here back to the parking lot—or for a slightly longer return, continue straight, eventually reaching Square Lake Road. From here turn right and walk the road 0.1 mile back to the park entrance.

Plans call for building trails around the lake and connecting to Camp Calvinwood and Coulter Creek, so there should soon be many more miles to explore. Trails here may also someday connect to the system of well-built and manicured trails within the McCormick Woods housing development to the north (currently open only to residents of the development), offering an extensive trail network.

GO FARTHER

The nearby South Kitsap Regional County Park (off Lund Avenue in Port Orchard, east of SR 16), while heavily developed with playfields, a skate park, and even a mini-railroad, has several miles of good trails for walking and running. The annual Hotfoot 5K Trail Race held in June is a great way to enjoy these trails.

14 **Manchester State Park**

DISTANCE:	1.9 miles of trails
ELEVATION GAIN:	Up to 150 feet
HIGH POINT:	90 feet
DIFFICULTY:	Easy
FITNESS:	Walkers, hikers
FAMILY-FRIENDLY:	Old access roads are suitable for jogging strollers; keep children close by near coastal bluffs and historic buildings. Some trails steep but fine for young children.
DOG-FRIENDLY:	On leash
AMENITIES:	Privy, picnic tables, water, camping (year round), interpretive displays
CONTACT/MAP:	Manchester State Park, (360) 871-4065, http://parks .state.wa.us/542/Manchester
GPS:	N47 34.674 W122 32.975
BEFORE YOU GO:	A Discover Pass is required to enter the park.

GETTING THERE

Driving: From State Route 16 in Port Orchard (milepost 25), follow Sedgewick Road east for 2.5 miles. Turn left onto Long Lake Road and proceed for 2.4 miles, turning right onto Mile Hill Drive. Continue east for 1.7 miles and turn left onto Colchester Drive. (From Southworth Ferry Terminal, follow Southworth Road west for 3.5 miles, turning right onto Colchester Drive.) Follow Colchester Drive 1.7 miles to Manchester, turning left onto Main Street and then immediately turning right onto Beach Drive. Continue on Beach Drive for 1.9 miles, turning right onto Hilldale Road. Proceed 0.7 mile into the state park to the day-use parking area.

Built at the turn of the twentieth century as a US Coast Artillery Harbor Defense station to protect Bremerton, this 111-acre state park property now protects 3400 feet of

1901-built Torpedo Warehouse

gorgeous shoreline on Rich Passage. Take to the park's trails to explore historic military buildings and soak up spectacular vistas that include Bainbridge and Blake islands and Mount Rainier.

GET MOVING

Two soft-surface trails, one paved trail, and one old service road (now a wide trail) diverge from the day-use parking area. Before hitting the trail, definitely explore the two adjacent historic buildings: the concrete Mining Casemate, set against a forested bluff, and the brick Torpedo Warehouse. Sitting in the open, the warehouse is a signature structure in the park. Built in 1901 to store torpedoes, it later served as an officer's club, barracks, mess hall, and finally as a picnic shelter.

The two soft-surface trails and an old road can be combined for short loop hikes. Consider following the old road first;
it travels along the coastline, granting good views across Rich
Passage to the undeveloped coastline on Bainbridge Island
occupied by Fort Ward, another old military base turned park.
At around 0.2 mile is a junction where an old road heads right,
eventually connecting to the two trails.

Continue straight, soon coming to Battery Mitchell. Then
pick up a singletrack trail and work your way around the
coastal ledges of Middle Point. The views are spectacular

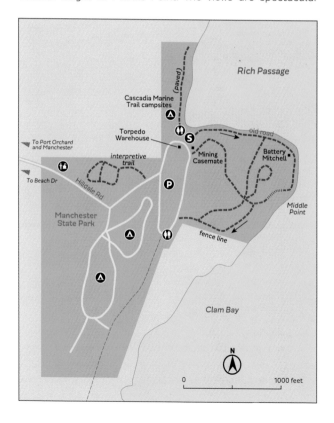

along this stretch of trail. Look out across Clam Bay to fish farms where eagles, gulls, seals, and sea lions are almost always in attendance. Then cast your attention farther beyond Orchard Point to snowy Mount Rainier hovering above the emerald undeveloped Blake Island.

The trail then turns inland and, utilizing stairs, climbs steeply, reaching the old road coming from the shoreline. From here walk the road to the right and then pick up the trail leading left to the parking lot. Or continue on the trail straight ahead, climbing a little higher along the park's boundary and beneath a canopy of big trees. At about a mile you'll return to the parking area.

The 0.2-mile paved trail near the old warehouse is worth a walk too. It passes a nice beach, picnic shelters, and Cascadia Marine Trail campsites; and hugs the shoreline, offering nice views of Middle Point and Bainbridge Island. And finally, walk a short distance up the park access road and find Manchester's other trail, a short and quiet interpretive trail.

15 Lions Park and Stephenson Canyon

DISTANCE:	2.4 miles of trails: 0.9 mile in Lions, 1.5 miles in the canyon
ELEVATION GAIN:	Up to 200 feet
HIGH POINT:	140 feet
DIFFICULTY:	Easy to moderate
FITNESS:	Walkers, hikers, runners
FAMILY-FRIENDLY:	Lions Park's lower loop is paved and flat, suitable for jogging strollers and wheelchairs. Stephenson Canyon trails are steep and may be difficult for young children.
DOG-FRIENDLY:	On leash

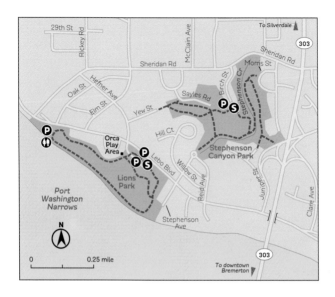

AMENITIES: Restrooms, picnic tables and shelter, water, and playground at Lions Park

CONTACT: City of Bremerton, www.bremertonwa.gov/210/Parks -Recreation

GPS: N 47 35.071 W 122 38.361

GETTING THERE

Driving: From downtown Bremerton, follow State Route 303 (Warren Avenue) north for 1.3 miles, turning right (after crossing the bridge) onto Clare Avenue. Follow Clare Avenue for 0.2 mile and turn right onto Lebo Boulevard. Proceed for 0.6 mile to Lions Park with parking on your left. Additional parking can be found 0.3 mile west on Lebo Boulevard.

Transit: Kitsap Transit #25 East Park stops at Lions Park.

Take an easy walk or run around the beautifully manicured grounds of Lions Park on Port Washington Narrows. Watch shorebirds in the nearby surf and clouds dancing off the jagged Olympic peaks in the distance. Then head up to a hidden

Stephenson Creek

canyon within a historic neighborhood where you can marvel at a tumbling creek and some remarkably big trees—all within Kitsap County's largest city.

Here's a chance to compare and contrast two distinctly different parks located minutes from each other. One is well landscaped with well-tended playfields, benches, and amenities. The other is a pocket wilderness that feels like it can be deep in the Olympics—not in Bremerton. Explore these two together or visit on separate occasions.

GET MOVING

From either parking area, walk onto the paved loop trail and begin enjoying one of Bremerton's most aesthetically pleasing parks. Lions Park was given a major makeover a few years back, which included restoring its 1900 feet of shoreline on Port Washington Narrows with natural vegetation; removing two ballfields; adding more trail distance; and adding a play area with orca whale sculptures.

The main trail makes a 0.7-mile loop around the park—or you can add 0.2 mile by taking an "upper" loop extension. On a sunny day, the views along this popular paved path are quite sublime, with Mount Rainier and Mount Constance in the Olympics clearly visible over waterways and neighborhoods.

GO FARTHER

From Lions Park you can walk to Stephenson Canyon, following signs that direct you from the loop trail. Walk up Stephenson Avenue for four blocks (carefully crossing Lebo Boulevard) to the Stephenson Avenue trailhead.

About 1.5 miles of trails traverse this 28.5-acre park protecting a deep ravine within the historic Sheridan Park Neighborhood. This neighborhood was developed by the Bremerton Housing Authority almost overnight in 1942 to supply housing to defense workers during World War II. This was a time of unprecedented growth in Bremerton, with its population topping out at 80,000 by 1945. Decades later the neighborhood and undeveloped canyon fell into neglect. Citizens came together to begin revitalizing the neighborhood, and Stephenson Canyon became a city park where a group of dedicated volunteers cleaned it up and built a trail system through it.

This trailhead is one of seven accessing the park. Walk up the narrow trail (rough in places) into a remarkably lush and wild ravine following alongside cascading Stephenson Creek. There are some big trees growing here, some of the oldest within the city. At 0.1 mile you'll come to a junction. Continue right along the creek, reaching another junction in 0.1 mile. Here you can veer right and drop into the ravine bottom, crossing the creek and hiking trails up and out of the ravine to the Morris, Morrison, and Callahan Street trailheads.

The trail to the left climbs steeply out of the ravine, reaching the Birch Street trailhead (the only trailhead of the park with parking, via Birch Street from Sheridan Road) near a greenhouse in 0.2 mile. From here follow a wide trail (old road) left and downhill, coming to another junction in about 0.1 mile. Turn left here, and in 0.1 mile you'll return to your first junction where you can head right and retrace your steps back to Lions Park.

16 Illahee Preserve Heritage Park

DISTANCE:	5 miles of trails
ELEVATION GAIN:	Up to 250 feet
HIGH POINT:	450 feet
DIFFICULTY:	Easy to Moderate
FITNESS:	Hikers, runners
FAMILY-FRIENDLY:	Well-groomed and marked trails suitable for children of all ages; trails are open to bikes
DOG-FRIENDLY:	On leash
AMENITIES:	Picnic tables
CONTACT/MAP:	Illahee Preserve Stewardship Committee, www.illaheepreserve.org
GPS:	N47 36.802 W122 37.363

GETTING THERE

Driving: From downtown Bremerton, follow State Route 303 (which goes from Warren Avenue to Wheaton Way) 3 miles north, turning right onto NE Riddell Road. Continue for 0.3 mile and turn left onto Almira Drive NE, proceeding 0.4 mile to the Illahee Preserve trailhead and parking area. (From Silverdale, follow SR 303 south for 5.4 miles, turning left onto NE Fuson Road. Continue for 0.3 mile, turning right onto Almira Drive NE, and reach the trailhead in another 0.1 mile.)

Aside from the main trailhead on Almira Drive NE, there is also a trailhead with limited parking at Thompson Lane NE off Riddell Road to the south; and trail access from the McWilliams Road Park and Ride.

Transit: Kitsap Transit route #17 Silverdale East stops at the main trailhead; Kitsap Transit route #15 McWilliams Shuttle stops at the trailhead at McWilliams Road Park and Ride.

The 545-acre forested Illahee Preserve is wedged between bustling Bremerton and Silverdale. The centerpiece of a nearly

Wood-chipped trail at Illahee Preserve

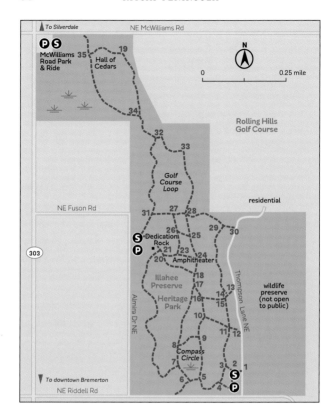

intact watershed within an urban area on Puget Sound, it was once slated for hundreds of homes. But concerned citizens rallied to preserve it—then worked hard to restore it and build an excellent trail system, transforming it into a wonderful greenbelt park.

This former DNR property was heavily neglected for decades, riddled with illegal dumping and dirt-biking. County officials and citizen groups like the Rotary Club and the Illahee Forest Stewardship Committee worked hard once the land became a county park in 2001 to restore it and construct an excellent trail system. Volunteers hauled away more than 85,000 pounds of garbage and twenty-two abandoned vehicles. These dedicated folks then proceeded to improve the park's trail system by closing poorly built paths—and improving other paths and building new ones. Many of the trails have been widened and their tread enhanced with wood chips, making a cushioned surface for running.

GET MOVING

Heavily wooded, Illahee makes for a good rainy-day hike. The trail system currently consists of more than 5 miles. Junctions are well marked with numbered posts, currently 34 in all. Take along a park map to help you negotiate the system.

Most of the preserve consists of mature second-growth Douglas firs and grand firs, but there are a few 200-plus-year-old trees here and there. While it's mostly a uniform forest, the map notes a few interesting areas worth checking out: The Compass Circle is a small, nearly circular, grassy wetland. The Amphitheater is a small ledgy area within deep timber. And the Hall of Cedars is exactly what you'd expect—but they're pretty small cedars, so don't expect a magnificent row of trees. Someday.

You can create a series of loops, up to a 3-mile hike by utilizing trails along the entire periphery. The section of trail between posts 7 and 22 at the southwest end of the park is particularly attractive.

Illahee is a Chinook jargon word meaning country, land, or place—and this place has even greater potential as a greenbelt. Conservationists are hoping to continue to expand the preserve by adding adjoining undeveloped (and threatened with development) parcels. If these lands can be secured, volunteers would like to build a trail along Illahee Creek to Puget Sound and another one to the Illahee State Park, also located on the sound. Visit www.thelostcontinent.org to learn how you can help make this a reality.

17 Clear Creek Trail

DISTANCE:	More than 7 miles of trails
ELEVATION GAIN:	Up to 200 feet
HIGH POINT:	180 feet
DIFFICULTY:	Easy
FITNESS:	Walkers, runners
FAMILY-FRIENDLY:	All but the Hospital Hill and Markwick trails within the system are jogging-stroller friendly and ADA-accessible. Much of the trail system is comprised of wide, well-groomed, hard-packed dirt tread. There are also paved and boardwalk sections.
DOG-FRIENDLY:	On leash
AMENITIES:	Restrooms, picnic tables
CONTACT/MAP:	Clear Creek Task Force, www.clearcreektrail.org
GPS:	N47 40.089 W122 40.900
BEFORE YOU GO:	Although the trail is well signed, do download and carry a copy of the trail map. And exercise caution, especially with children, crossing Silverdale Way and Myhre Place near the SR 303 (Waaga Way) Interchange. This is a busy and potentially dangerous crossing, with poor markings and plenty of inattentive drivers. A pedestrian overpass would make this interchange a whole lot safer.

GETTING THERE

Driving: From Bremerton, drive State Route 3 north to Silverdale, taking exit 45. Turn right on Kitsap Mall Boulevard, then immediately left onto NW Randall Way. Continue for 1 mile and turn left onto Silverdale Way. Proceed north 0.9 mile, turning left into Silverdale Rotary Gateway Park.

Other good access points with ample parking for this trail system include Old Mill Park on Bucklin Hill Road and Silverdale Waterfront Park on Byron Street in Old Town Silverdale.

Boardwalk along the North Wetlands Trail

Transit: Kitsap Transit #36 Ridgetop services Silverdale Rotary Gateway Park. Kitsap Transit #25 Old Town Shuttle services the Silverdale Waterfront and Old Mill parks.

A network of trails actually, the Clear Creek Trail consists of more than 7 miles of paved and unpaved trails in a greenbelt located smack dab right in the middle of Kitsap County's largest retail center. From a waterfront park on Dyes Inlet to a riparian corridor along salmon-rearing Clear Creek to an extensive wetland system in a historic farm belt, this is one of the finest urban trails on the Kitsap Peninsula.

Spend an hour or all day walking or running this excellent trail system. While the heart of the trail brushes right up against busy shopping centers, the forested corridor makes it feel like you're in a much less developed area. And while the trail is well used, there are plenty of sections offering quiet ambling. The section of trail north of the Waaga Way Interchange—a section best accessed from the Silverdale Rotary Gateway Park—offers some of the best walking and running.

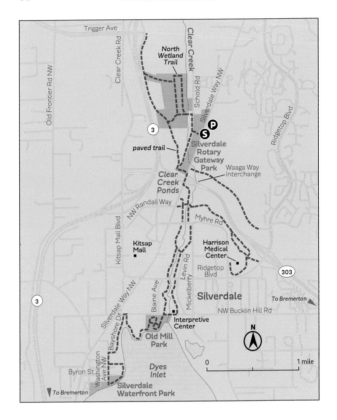

GET MOVING

From the Silverdale Rotary Gateway Park trailhead, follow a closed road (now trail) 0.3 mile to the Clear Creek Trail. Then walk north on the paved trail for 1.2 miles through old farmland (currently being restored to wetland marshes). Several side trails divert from the paved path, allowing for loop options. The North Wetland Trail is exceptionally nice, making a 0.8-mile loop mainly on boardwalk through a bird- and wildlife-rich grassy wetland in the Clear Creek Valley.

South of SR 303 you can follow a soft-surface trail on both sides of Clear Creek for 1 mile south to Old Mill Park. There are several road crossings (good crosswalks) and bridges spanning the creek, allowing for shorter loops or figure-eight hiking. Points of interest along the way include the Clear Creek Ponds (working retention ponds), the small estuary near Dyes Inlet, and the Interpretive Center, housed in a red barn. If the center is open, drop in and learn about the ongoing restoration efforts in this watershed. Also learn about the Clear Creek Task Force (CCTF), which is responsible for creating this greenbelt. Formed in 1993 under the aegis of the Great Peninsula Conservancy (see sidebar "Creating Great Parks and Trails on the Great Peninsula"), the CCTF is comprised of local citizens, conservation groups, businesses, and service organizations.

South of NW Bucklin Hill Road you can continue on the Clear Creek Trail. Here at a brand-new bridge and pedestrian crossing, enter the Old Mill Park where you can mill around on some short side trails leading to displays and remnants of the sawmill that once occupied this now tranquil spot.

South of the park the trail hugs pretty shoreline along Dyes Inlet and crosses (via an easement) the grounds of the Silverdale Beach Best Western hotel. At 0.5 mile from the park, the trail comes back to NW Bucklin Hill Road, then continues 0.7 mile south to the Silverdale Waterfront Park. Mainly following sidewalks along Bayshore Drive, Washington Avenue NW, and Lowell Street, it's a pleasant route along the shoreline (which during low tides exposes quite a large mud and salt flat).

East of Randall Way is yet another section of the Clear Creek Trail—a 0.6-mile extension that climbs (not suitable for strollers) a small forested ridge to the Harrison Medical Center. En route you'll pass a giant grand fir, the foundation of an old homestead, and a decent view of Dyes Inlet, the Olympics, and Green Mountain. In the attractive woods near the medical center a spur veers left, allowing you to make a small loop (with a short sidewalk section on Ridgetop Boulevard).

| 18 | **Big Tree Trail** |

DISTANCE:	1.4 miles round-trip
DIFFICULTY:	Moderate
ELEVATION GAIN:	200 feet
HIGH POINT:	400 feet
FITNESS:	Hikers
FAMILY-FRIENDLY:	Trail suitable for hikers of all ages and abilities
DOG-FRIENDLY:	Dogs prohibited
CONTACT/MAP:	Mountaineers Foundation, http://mountaineersfoundation.org/ no map available online
AMENITIES:	None; respect preserve buildings/not open to the public
GPS:	N47 35.331 W122 43.995
BEFORE YOU GO:	The Rhododendron Preserve is open daylight hours only; please sign in with the caretaker or leave a note on your dashboard saying you are visiting the preserve.

GETTING THERE

Driving: From Bremerton, follow Kitsap Way west, turning left onto Northlake Road. In 1.1 miles turn left onto Seabeck Highway. (From Silverdale, follow Chico Way south, turning right onto Northlake Road. In 0.4 mile turn right onto Seabeck Highway.) Continue 0.9 mile, turning left into the preserve entrance. Drive past a private entrance, reaching the parking area in 0.1 mile.

Protecting some of the oldest and biggest trees remaining in the Puget Trough, including one Douglas fir with a diameter over 30 feet, this quiet nature preserve sits at the confluence

KITSAP PENINSULA FIRST PEOPLES

Long before American, European, and Asian settlers homesteaded on the Kitsap Peninsula, the region was home to the Suquamish people. "People of the clear salt water," the Suquamish depended upon the area's salmon, seafood, plants, and game for their livelihoods. They lived in shed-roofed plank houses during the winter, and their major winter village was at Old Man House on the shore of Agate Pass. They were renowned basket and canoe makers.

Their first contact with non-natives was in 1792 when British Captain George Vancouver surveyed the area. Great, disruptive, and destructive changes to the tribe would soon follow. By 1855, they had relinquished title to most of their lands, but retained fishing and hunting rights and a reservation at Port Madison. Many Suquamish today continue to live on the Port Madison Indian Reservation in the towns of Suquamish and Indianola. And despite past moves to assimilate and deprive them of certain aspects of their culture, the tribe has kept its culture and heritage strong—as well as become a driving economic presence on the Kitsap Peninsula. Their economic arm, Port Madison Enterprises, is the second-largest private-sector employer in Kitsap County. They own and manage the Suquamish Clearwater Casino Resort as well as the Suquamish Museum (http:/suquamishmuseum.org) where you can learn more about their most famous tribal member, Chief Seattle.

According to tribal sources, Seattle was born in 1786 at the Old Man House (others say he was born in 1780 on Blake Island) to a Suquamish Chief and Duwamish mother. Seattle would eventually achieve status as chief of the Suquamish and a confederation of Duwamish bands. He would watch an influx of non-natives settle into his ancestral lands and great changes wrought upon his people. He feared that a military conflict with the United States government could not be won, and signed the 1855 Treaty of Point Elliott with the US government, relinquishing title to Suquamish lands. Some of the other Puget Sound tribes were angered by this and past treaties, and waged battles against the US military and area settlers. Chief Seattle kept his people from participating. And for this, and long friendships with settlers along Elliott Bay (including Doc Maynard), the founding fathers named the new city growing on the bay after Chief Seattle.

Chief Seattle continued to live in Suquamish, but frequently traveled to the city bearing his name. He died in 1866 and was buried in Suquamish. His grave can be visited and, along with other cultural sites, is just a short walk from the Suquamish Museum.

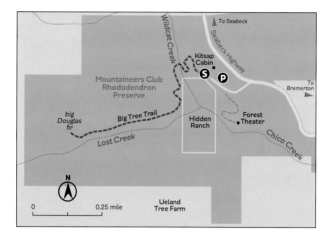

of two salmon-bearing creeks. The century-old preserve's most interesting feature, however, is its 1923 outdoor theater—home of the Mountaineers Players, one of the oldest nonprofit theater groups in the country.

The Mountaineers Foundation, which owns the Rhododendron Preserve, and the Mountaineers, which owns the surrounding lands, are currently studying options for the Hidden Ranch section of this parcel, including prospects for an outdoor education center. Both organizations have steadily worked to expand the entire property. Starting in 1915 with 74 acres, the preserve now encompasses 460 acres. The groups continue to acquire adjacent tracts.

GET MOVING

From the parking area, walk 0.1 mile west on a narrow dirt road, past the caretakers' home (don't forget to sign in) and several other buildings, coming to a gate. The road beyond the gate heads to the historic Hidden Ranch, and is currently closed to the public.

The Big Tree Trail takes off to the right of the gated road. Beneath rhodies (spectacular in May and early June) and

The big Douglas fir of the Big Tree Trail

a canopy held up by giant old firs, the way descends into a lush ravine where Wildcat and Lost creeks come together to form Chico Creek. The preserve helps maintain the ecological integrity of this watershed, an important salmon-spawning run. Here at the confluence are more than 70 forested acres that have never been cut.

The trail crosses Wildcat Creek on a bridge made from a large fallen old-growth giant, and meanders beside big maples and cedars. It then bends left and climbs over a small rise before heading across the Lost Creek floodplain, passing beautiful old trees. Hikers of all ages will get a kick out of the encouraging signs along the way, including "Keep Going" and "Almost There."

At 0.7 mile from the parking area, reach the massive Douglas fir that just may be the biggest one on the Kitsap Peninsula. Admire it and then return, remembering you have a short climb out of the ravine.

GO FARTHER

Near the historic 1917 Kitsap Cabin is a much newer treehouse that kids will love exploring. And if a show is not in session, definitely check out the nearby outdoor Forest Theater. Walk the theater path 0.3 mile through a thick canopy of mature firs and showy rhododendrons. Carved into a hillside and surrounded by old-growth firs and big fern boughs, the terraced amphitheater is a beautiful natural setting for watching a play. The Mountaineers Players perform several shows throughout spring and summer. The theater also conducts summer camps for children. Packages include transportation from the Bremerton ferry dock for enrolled children from the Seattle area. For information, visit www.foresttheater.com.

19 Ueland Tree Farm Trails

DISTANCE:	0.8 mile singletrack and more than 14 miles of woods roads
ELEVATION GAIN:	Up to 900 feet
HIGH POINT:	1025 feet
DIFFICULTY:	Easy to moderate

FITNESS:	Walkers, hikers, runners
FAMILY-FRIENDLY:	Forest road trails can accommodate jogging strollers, albeit bumpy in spots; use caution with young children near waterfall
DOG-FRIENDLY:	Off-leash permitted
AMENITIES:	Privy
CONTACT/MAP:	Ueland Tree Farm, www.uelandtreefarm.com
GPS:	N47 34.800 W122 43.082
BEFORE YOU GO:	The tree farm is actively managed; be mindful of vehicles and equipment accessing timber harvest areas and on-site quarries. Roads and section of forest are subject to temporary closures during harvests. Respect all rules and regulations.

GETTING THERE

Driving: From State Route 3 in Bremerton, follow Kitsap Way west for 1.5 miles, bearing left onto Northlake Way. Continue for 0.5 mile and make a hard left onto Lebers Lane NW. Proceed 0.2 mile to the trailhead. From Silverdale, follow SR 3 south to the Chico Way exit. Turn right onto Chico Way and proceed for 0.6 mile. Then turn right onto Northlake Way and drive 0.9 mile, turning right onto Lebers Lane.

Transit: Kitsap Transit Route #12 Silverdale West stops on Northlake Way near Lebers Lane.

A 2500-acre family-owned, sustainably managed tree farm open to the public for non-motorized recreation (including mountain bikes and horses), the Ueland Tree Farm is also a key parcel in an emerging greenbelt and long-distance trail network on the Kitsap Peninsula. While the forest's two trails are in essence timber roads, they offer quiet hiking and a few surprises—a waterfall and views of the Olympic mountains and Hood Canal—along the way.

These forestlands have been in productive use since Washington attained statehood in 1889, the year the Port Blakely Company purchased them. The Uelands began acquiring these lands in 2004. Under their management they put conservation easements on parcels along Lost and Chico creeks,

Hood Canal view from a 1025-foot knoll

and established floating (meaning that their alignments may shift as harvesting progresses) trail corridors. These corridors are the roads that make up the Lost Creek and Chico Creek trails, which will someday be part of a long-distance trail from Jorsted Park to Newberry Hill Heritage Park.

GET MOVING

From the recently expanded parking lot, head right on the Chico Trail. Heading through mature cedars, this wide and well-built trail crosses a powerline swath before making a short, steep climb to a level area that has been selectively cut. The trail follows along a deep, forested ravine cradling Dickerson Creek.

After about 0.8 mile the Chico Trail reaches road U1100 and follows it right. Walk the road for 0.25 mile and come to an unmarked junction. Here a trail takes off right for a couple hundred feet into a tangle of Scotch broom to an old dam on Dickerson Creek and small waterfall spilling into a tight ravine below it. Be very careful here viewing the waterfall.

The Chico Trail (U1100) continues west, reaching a junction with the Lost Creek Trail (forest road) in another couple hundred feet, about 1.1 miles from the trailhead.

If you're looking for longer hiking and running options than the waterfall route, you can continue left on the Chico Trail (now following road U1110). Head south on this route through a recent cut, passing many side spur roads (which

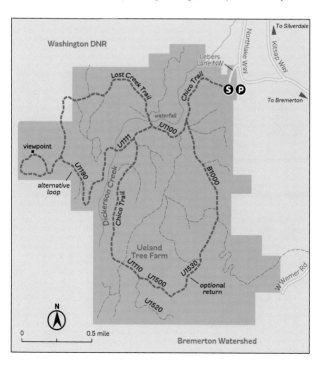

are generally signed); and eventually gently climb to attractive mature forest along a small ridge.

At 1.5 miles from the Lost Creek Trail junction, the Chico Trail bends left (east) to follow U1500. Continue another 0.2 mile to the junction with U1520. Here the Chico Trail bears right to follow U1520 for 0.6 mile, ending at the forest boundary. Skip that section and instead either retrace your route or return via U1500, U1530, and B1000 for a pleasant 1.3-mile route looping back to the Chico Trail singletrack.

Or, from the trail junction near the waterfall you can take the Lost Creek Trail, which follows U1100, skirting a wetland and coming to the tree farm boundary at 1.1 miles from the junction. Keep walking, passing through WA DNR forest and reentering the Ueland Tree Farm at 1.4 miles. Gradually climbing, U1100 eventually splits at 1.9 miles. Go either way for a 0.7-mile loop, reaching the forest's 1025-foot high point and—thanks to a cut—sweeping views of Hood Canal and Mounts Constance, Buckhorn, and Jupiter. Then return the way you came, or make a loop by following U1190 to U1111 to U1110 for 1.6 miles back to the trail junction.

20 Newberry Hill Heritage Park

DISTANCE:	12 miles of trails
ELEVATION GAIN:	Up to 200 feet
HIGH POINT:	525 feet
DIFFICULTY:	Easy to moderate
FITNESS:	Hikers, runners
FAMILY-FRIENDLY:	Excellent, but be aware of mountain bikers on some trails; the Wildlife Trail, with its observation deck near an extensive wetland, is a great kid-friendly trail
DOG-FRIENDLY:	On leash
CONTACT/MAP:	Friends of Heritage Hill Park, www.friendsofnhhp.com
GPS:	N47 38.062 W122 45.319

Wetland Complex along the Wildlife Trail

GETTING THERE

Driving: From State Route 3 in Silverdale, follow Newberry Hill Road west for 2.3 miles, turning left onto School Road (signed for Klahowya Secondary School). Proceed south for 0.1 mile to the park's north (main) trailhead, with parking alongside the road. Do not use the Klahowya Secondary School parking lot during school hours (it's okay to park there when school is not in session).

For the Holly Gate (southern) trailhead: From Bremerton, follow Kitsap Way west, turning left onto Northlake Road. In 1.1 miles turn left onto Seabeck Highway. (From Silverdale, follow Chico Way south, turning right onto Northlake Road. In 0.4 mile turn right onto Seabeck Highway.) Continue west on Seabeck Highway for 3 miles to the intersection with Holly Road. The trailhead is on the right.

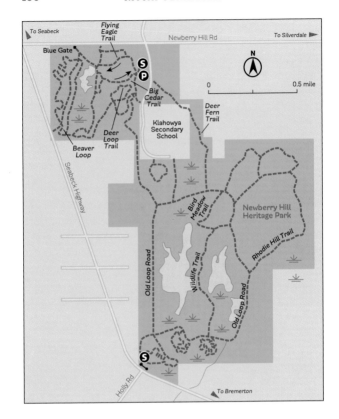

Parking is limited at the Holly Gate, but it offers access to the park from the south, providing for a shorter hike to the Wildlife and Rhodie Hill trails.

One of Kitsap County's largest and newest parks, Newberry Hill Heritage Park offers 12 miles of well-maintained, non-motorized interconnecting trails. While some of these trails traverse recently cutover forest lands, others cross wetland complexes where you can admire mature trees and observe abundant wildlife. For runners, there's enough trail mileage here to do some serious training.

Transferred to Kitsap County Parks from the Washington Department of Natural Resources in 2009, the 1100-acre Newberry Hill Heritage Park had been extensively logged over the decades. But within this sprawling property that surrounds the Klahowya Secondary School campus (carved out of the parcel) are pockets of mature forest and several large wetland areas.

There are over 12 miles of well-marked trails within the park, including some that were former skid roads. An active volunteer group, the Friends of Newberry Hill Heritage Park, has worked hard on maintaining and mapping these trails as well as being good stewards of this property. The park is currently unfunded, so these volunteers have been integral to the park's development and upkeep. And while this tract is no longer managed for timber production, selective cutting is still being carried out here to promote good forest health.

GET MOVING

With a map in hand (sometimes available at trailhead kiosk— better to download one), head out and explore the park, crafting your own routes and loops, from short lunch-break strolls to all-day romps. The trails and junctions are well marked. For a nice starter loop, from the north trailhead, consider hiking the Flying Eagle Trail to the Beaver Loop, returning on the Big Cedar Trail. It's an easy 2.4-mile loop to and around a large beaver pond, mostly on hiker-only trails, with boardwalks over wet areas. Along the way you'll see rhododendrons, evergreen huckleberry, and some mature timber. There are some big Doug firs on the Big Cedar Trail, but you'll be hard-pressed to find a cedar big or small.

The 0.8-mile hiker-only Wildlife Trail is perhaps the nicest trail within the park. It travels through attractive groves of tall trees along the eastern shoreline of a very large pond and wetland complex. An observation deck offers good bird-watching. To access this trail, you can hike the 0.8-mile Deer Fern Trail to the Old Loop Road, then walk 0.1 mile east to the Bird Meadow Trail, which leads 0.4 mile to the Wildlife Trail. Another option is to continue 0.25 mile farther on the Old Loop Road to the beginning of the Wildlife Trail, marked with a wildlife-etched mailbox that may hold a supply of trail maps. You can follow the Wildlife Trail back to the Old Loop Road, from where you can return to the Deer Fern Trail in either direction. The Old Loop Road is 2.6 miles long, and it's about the same distance to return, either left or right.

Another trail to consider is the Rhodie Hill Trail, which loops 1.1 mile off the Old Loop Road, giving you an option to increase not only your mileage but also your elevation gain. This trail climbs about 150 feet, passing through groves of madronas and rhodies and a small wetland.

As noted above, the shortest approach to this trail is via a spur road/trail connecting the Old Loop Road with the south trailhead on the Seabeck Highway near its junction with Holly Road.

21 Green Mountain

DISTANCE:	5.2 miles round-trip
ELEVATION GAIN:	1100 feet
HIGH POINT:	1639 feet
DIFFICULTY:	Moderately difficult
FITNESS:	Hikers, runners
FAMILY-FRIENDLY:	Trails fine for older kids; be aware of bikes, motorbikes, and horses
DOG-FRIENDLY:	On leash
AMENITIES:	Privy, picnic tables

Green Mountain's summit offers a nice view of the Seattle skyline.

CONTACT/MAP:	Department of Natural Resources, South Puget Sound Region, (360) 825-1631, www.dnr.wa.gov
GPS:	N47 33.117 W122 49.591
BEFORE YOU GO:	A Discover Pass is required to enter the state forest. **NOTE:** Logging through 2017 will temporarily close trails within Green Mountain.

GETTING THERE

Driving: From Bremerton, follow Kitsap Way west, turning left onto Northlake Road. In 1.1 miles turn left onto Seabeck Highway. (From Silverdale, follow Chico Way south, turning right onto Northlake Road. In 0.4 mile turn right onto Seabeck Highway.) Continue west on Seabeck Highway for 3 miles, turning left onto NW Holly Road. Proceed for 4.1 miles and turn left onto Tahuya Lake Road. Continue south 1.2 miles, bearing left onto Gold Creek Road, to reach the trailhead on your left in 1.8 miles. Parking is at the trailhead.

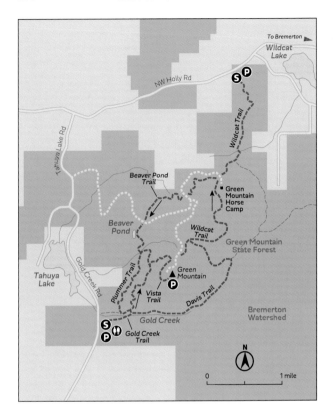

Climb to the top of the Kitsap Peninsula's second-highest peak, and you'll be rewarded with good views of Puget Sound, the Seattle skyline, and Mount Rainier. Then return on a route taking you to a cascading creek and views of the Olympics. Though Green Mountain is a good destination year round, come in late spring when the forest is abloom with pink rhododendron boughs.

Along with neighboring 1761-foot Gold Mountain, 1639-foot Green Mountain makes up the rooftop of the Kitsap Peninsula. Granted, these peaks' elevations aren't exactly nosebleed-inducing. But standing above the surrounding low country, right in the middle of the peninsula, both summits offer eagle's-eye views of a lot of saltwater and snowcapped mountains.

Gold Mountain is within the closed-to-the-public Bremerton watershed and off-limits to hikers. But Green Mountain is accessed by several well-maintained trails and surrounded by more than 6000 acres of state forest. However, the trails in Green Mountain State Forest are open to motorcycles, making them less than ideal for hiking. The good news is that foot traffic dominates here, and WA DNR is in the process of closing several of these trails to motorized use. Motorcyclists have free rein at nearby Tahuya State Forest, so having some non-motorized trails at Green Mountain seems a fair compromise, bringing Green Mountain a step closer to becoming Bremerton's Tiger Mountain.

GET MOVING

Starting from an elevation of 650 feet, the Gold Creek Trail (an old woods road) leads you through a thick tunnel of vegetation. The way then bends right, following alongside Gold Creek which tumbles below in a ravine. At 0.6 mile the trail crosses the creek over a bridge and meets a woods road. The woods road, recently converted to the Davis Trail, allows access to the summit while active logging closes the main routes. Turn left, hiking away from the creek, and soon encounter another junction. The trail left is the Plummer Trail, your return route for this loop hike. Hang a right, staying on the Gold Creek Trail, and steadily climb.

The trail ascends through a leathery dark-green understory of salal, bearberry, madrona, and rhododendron, and then splits. Either branch works—they meet again soon enough. Limited views of the Olympics tease through the trees. At 1.6 miles reach a junction with the Beaver Pond Trail (signed for Green Mountain Camp) left, your return route. But first the summit—so continue right, coming to a junction with the Wildcat Trail at 1.9 miles.

Continue right, now on the Vista Trail, coming to a privy and parking lot (only open weekends in the summer) at 2.1 miles. Stay on the Vista Trail, passing ledges, rhodies, old roads, and picnic tables, reaching Green Mountain's rocky summit at 2.4 miles. The summit ledges are edged with a chain-link fence, good for keeping kids safe, not for aesthetics. And the view is growing in (it's a working forest) but still pretty decent. Look eastward over Bremerton, Puget Sound, and the Seattle skyline, and out to the Cascades. Mount Rainier's summit can be seen over Gold Mountain.

When ready to head back, retrace your steps 0.8 mile to the Beaver Pond Trail junction. Bear right here, descending 0.3 mile to a junction with the Plummer Trail. The Beaver Pond (more a grassland than wetland) is about 0.2 mile to the right, just after crossing a bridge over a cascading creek, a worthwhile side trip. Otherwise head left on the Plummer Trail.

The Plummer Trail climbs 125 feet, skirting a recent cut, then descends, crossing a logging road and taking in good views of the Tahuya Lake and the Olympic mountains west. At 2.1 miles from the summit, bear left at a junction (the trail right leads to private property) and follow Gold Creek for 0.1 mile back to the Gold Creek Trail. Turn right, and retrace familiar tread 0.6 mile back to the trailhead.

GO FARTHER

Green Mountain can also be hiked from the north, starting at the Wildcat trailhead (on NW Holly Road) and following the 4-mile Wildcat Trail. However, this route is quite rocky in spots and receives heavy ATV use. A good extended loop hiking option is to follow the Wildcat Trail from the Vista Trail junction north for 2 miles (passing recent cuts offering excellent views) to the Beaver Pond Trail junction near the Green

Mountain Horse Camp. Then follow the pleasant Beaver Pond Trail through new cuts, attractive forest, and wetlands 2.4 miles to the Plummer Trail. This extended loop will give you a 9.1-mile total hiking tally.

22 Anderson Landing Preserve

DISTANCE:	2 miles of trails
ELEVATION GAIN:	225 feet
HIGH POINT:	225 feet
DIFFICULTY:	Moderate
FITNESS:	Hikers
FAMILY-FRIENDLY:	Trails are narrow and steep, best for older children
DOG-FRIENDLY:	On leash; be cautious near bluff tops
CONTACT/MAP:	Kitsap County Parks, www.kitsapgov.com/parks/Parks /Pages/regionalparks/anderson_landing_preserve.htm
GPS:	N47 39.680 W122 45.702

GETTING THERE

Driving: From Silverdale Way in Silverdale, follow NW Anderson Hill Road west for 3.7 miles. Then turn right onto Warren Road NW and proceed for 0.2 mile to the trailhead. Parking is at the trailhead.

A pocket preserve providing access to a beautiful stretch of Hood Canal coastline, Anderson Landing also provides stunning bluff-top views and nice walking through a ferny gulch. Take to 2 miles of trails over rugged topography that was once logged but never developed, providing for a sliver of wild just minutes from shopping malls and office parks.

While Anderson Landing is a mere 82 acres, it seems larger. Protecting the mouth of Anderson Creek on Hood Canal, much of the park consists of a deep ravine and steep slopes, giving it an isolated feeling. As with several other

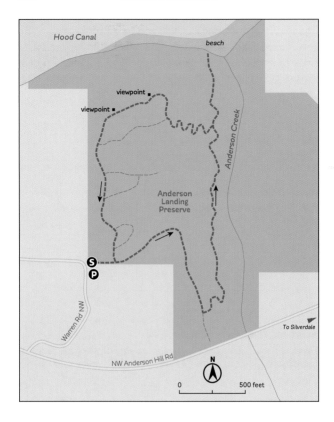

Kitsap County Parks, the trails here were built by volunteers, who also hauled out trash left from years of illegal dumping from unenlightened souls.

GET MOVING

For a nice 1.4-mile loop hike, start hiking down the main trail, once part of Anderson Hill Road. After a short distance on crumbling and duff-covered asphalt, come to a junction. You can go either way for the loop, but stay right for an easier descent on the old road. Rounding steep slopes, the old road brings you to another junction. The way straight peters out on NW Anderson Hill Road (no parking), so turn left on a bona fide trail that descends into the lush ravine containing Anderson Creek. Like many other geographical features on the Kitsap Peninsula, this creek's name testifies to the large numbers of folks of Scandinavian descent that homesteaded here.

Follow the creek downstream, soon coming to an unmarked but obvious junction. You'll be returning left; for now continue straight another 0.1 mile, passing a small dam, arriving at the end of the trail on a small forested bluff. When the tide is low, clamber over some roots and explore the beach and tidal flats, with views across Hood Canal to the tip of the Toandos Peninsula and the Olympic summits Mount Walker, The Brothers, and Mount Jupiter.

After you've explored the beach, retrace your steps to the last junction and head right, steeply climbing out of the ravine via a series of short switchbacks. The way weaves through

Olympic Mountains view from extensive tidal flats on Hood Canal

head-high ferns and passes some big maples and firs. Once upon the bluff top, you reach another junction. Stay on the trail to the right (the one left takes a shorter route) and come to an overlook offering limited views over the shore and canal. Continue down the trail a short distance and come to a much better viewpoint at the edge of a slide. Stay back from the edge and watch children and dogs while enjoying this bluff-top vista.

The trail then bends left and heads south, passing four more junctions on the left; these are the endpoints of two short loops, if you're interested in tacking on a bit more distance.

Eventually reaching the main (old road) trail, turn right to return to your vehicle.

23 Guillemot Cove Nature Reserve

DISTANCE:	4 miles of trails
ELEVATION GAIN:	350 feet
HIGH POINT:	350 feet
DIFFICULTY:	Moderate
FITNESS:	Hikers
FAMILY-FRIENDLY:	Some trails are a little steep, but otherwise a very kid-friendly park, with a large beach and a cedar stump house
DOG-FRIENDLY:	Dogs prohibited
CONTACT/MAP:	Kitsap County Parks, www.kitsapgov.com/parks/Parks/Pages/regionalparks/guillemot_cove_county_park.htm
GPS:	N47 36.955 W122 54.519

GETTING THERE

Driving: From State Route 3 in Silverdale, follow Newberry Hill Road west for 3 miles, turning right onto the Seabeck Highway. Continue for 5 miles, turning right onto Miami Beach Road (no kidding). After 0.9 mile, bear left onto Stavis Bay

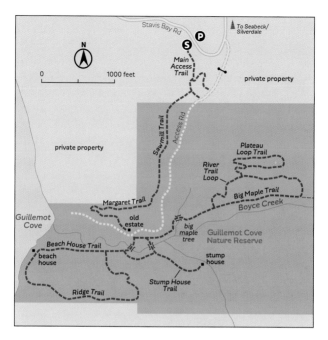

Road, following it for 4.5 miles to the Guillemot Cove Nature Reserve. Park on the right; the trail begins across the road.

One of the most beautiful spots on the Kitsap Peninsula, this county nature preserve protects almost 200 acres of stunning beach and stately forest on Hood Canal. Hike to a secluded cove teeming with seabirds and stare out at The Brothers, looming high above and directly across the canal. Explore groves of giant maples and showy rhododendrons, tunnels of evergreen huckleberry, and an old and intriguing stump house.

A former private estate on a quiet corner of Hood Canal, Guillemot Cove is now one of the crown jewels of Kitsap County Parks. Managed as a nature preserve, its trails are

Guillemot Cove from the old beach house

hiker-only, and kids will love the diversity and surprises this property has to offer.

GET MOVING

There are several hiking options, but all involve first hiking the Main Access Trail, Sawmill Trail, and Margaret Trail. Since this is a downhill hike to start, save energy for the 350-foot climb on the return.

On good tread, follow the Main Access Trail into a pleasant mature forest crowded with thick rows of evergreen huckleberry and rhododendrons. Bear right at two junctions with side trails; these lead short distances to the gated access road (an alternative route for your return hike). The trail you are on becomes the Sawmill Trail and continues a descent, soon passing through a beautiful flat of alders garnished with bouquets of ferns.

The trail eventually bends right and becomes the Margaret Trail. It then drops sharply into a cool ravine shaded by cedar, hemlock, and the occasional yew, and switchbacks east. Pass a decaying residence, and at 1 mile emerge in the heart of the old estate, reaching a barn in surrounding pasture. An information kiosk presents your hiking options.

The best choice is to cross the Boyce Creek bridge on the Beach House Trail, taking a right at its junction with the Stump House Trail. Walk along Boyce Creek and stay right at two more junctions making up the Ridge Trail. At 0.3 mile from the kiosk (1.3 miles from the trailhead), reach the old beach house overlooking Guillemot Cove. And what a beach! The Brothers, perhaps the most identifiable of all Olympic peaks, tower directly above Hood Canal. Five hundred feet deep and a mile across, Hood Canal is Washington's grand fjord.

At low tide Boyce Creek slithers across a muddy oyster bar. Scores of shorebirds scamper for succulent oyster shooters. Bald eagles sit watch on tall firs on the water's edge. Explore the rocky and mucky beach, but be mindful of delicate critters exposed to your crushing feet at low tide. And, while you're enjoying this special place, you may be thinking, "What's a guillemot?" It's a seabird that looks a bit like a penguin that can frequently be seen here wading in the surf.

After savoring the shoreline serenity, consider these other hiking options. During a low tide you can walk the beach south for a couple of miles. This shoreline is part of WA DNR's Stavis Natural Resources Conservation Area, which protects over 5200 acres of important habitat, including some of the oldest forest on the Kitsap Peninsula.

The Ridge Trail makes a 0.5-mile loop near the beach house along the boundary with the Stavis NRCA. After climbing 200 feet, it steeply descends, passing some big trees along the way.

The Stump House Trail leads 0.25 mile to a cedar stump house, a domicile to a desperado during the Depression.

Children will love this gnome-like setting. You can return via a spur leading back to the barn.

The 0.4-mile Big Maple Trail takes off from the barn, following alongside Boyce Creek and passing a gigantic bigleaf maple. You can return via the 0.2-mile River Trail Loop.

And the new Plateau Trail, leaving from the River Trail Loop, climbs 100 feet, making a small loop through second-growth timber. It'll add 0.4 mile to your hiking tally if you decide to check it out.

24 Poulsbo's Fish Park

DISTANCE:	1.5 miles of trails
ELEVATION GAIN:	50 feet
HIGH POINT:	60 feet
DIFFICULTY:	Easy
FITNESS:	Walkers
FAMILY-FRIENDLY:	Wide, smooth, fairly level pedestrian-only trails and long boardwalks make this park a good choice for young children; some trails are ADA-accessible
DOG-FRIENDLY:	On leash
AMENITIES:	Privy, benches, interpretive displays, bike racks, amphitheater, picnic tables
CONTACT/MAP:	City of Poulsbo Parks and Recreation, www.cityofpoulsbo.com/parks/parks/fish_park.htm
GPS:	N47 44.862 W122 39.190

GETTING THERE

Driving: From Bremerton, follow State Route 3 north, taking the Finn Hill Road exit. Turn right and follow Finn Hill Road east for 0.5 mile to Viking Avenue. Continue straight through the junction, now on Lindvig Way NW, for 0.1 mile, then turn left into the park.

From Kingston, follow SR 307 (Bond Road) to SR 305. Continue straight through the junction, still on Bond Road, for

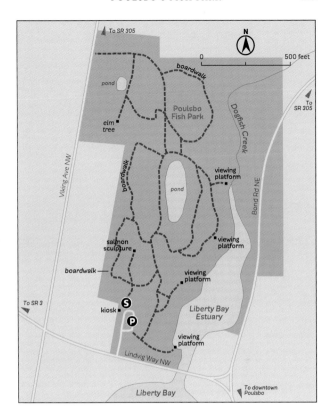

0.5 mile and turn right on Lindvig Way NW. Proceed for 0.1 mile, turning right into the park.

Transit: Kitsap Transit #32 Poulsbo-Silverdale, Kitsap Transit #43 Viking Avenue, and Kitsap Transit #44 Poulsbo Central all stop near the park.

A small park in the heart of a small but growing city, Poulsbo's Fish Park with its many amenities is sure to make a splash with you. While only 40 acres, the park is laced with a network of nature trails and boardwalks along a wildlife-rich estuary,

A boardwalk winds through Poulsbo's Fish Park.

one of the best places in the area to watch spawning salmon. There's history here, too—the site of a Suquamish cedar plank house, and a Norwegian immigrant homestead.

In the 1890s Steffen and Sigried Larson with their three sons arrived from Norway (like so many of Poulsbo's early homesteaders) to settle and work this land. One hundred years later, an old pond and mature American elm (a tree native to the eastern United States) are all that remain testifying to the family's tenure here.

GET MOVING

Walk the park's trails in no particular order, stopping to read interpretive panels and pausing to listen for and spot native critters. The trails are short, but there's plenty to observe—so take your time wandering around this park.

The first thing that'll grab your attention here is the giant salmon sculpture on a small knoll. But this isn't a typical sculpture—this 8-foot-long salmon was constructed from hundreds of pieces of driftwood by local artist Travis Foreman. It's a fitting symbol for this park that celebrates fish, nature, and restoration.

A former homestead, much of this park now sprouts regenerative growth, mostly native plants too, thanks to park volunteers removing most of the invasive species.

Volunteers did the majority of trail and boardwalk construction here, too, including two long boardwalks, five bridges, and four viewing platforms. The latter offer glimpses of Dogfish Creek and the Liberty Bay Estuary, great places for observing salmon.

And what's a dogfish? It's a small shark, once prized by early settlers for its oil, used for greasing logging skid roads. Liberty Bay was originally named Dogfish Bay by the early settlers—but the state legislature didn't care much for the name, prompting the name change.

GO FARTHER

If you'd like to do some walking alongside Liberty (Dogfish) Bay, head over to American Legion Park on Front Street. Here you can walk a short boardwalk to the Liberty Bay Waterfront Park. It's a short walk, long on good views.

25 North Kitsap Heritage Park

DISTANCE:	More than 10 miles of trails
ELEVATION GAIN:	Up to 275 feet
HIGH POINT:	325 feet
DIFFICULTY:	Easy to moderate
FITNESS:	Walkers, hikers, runners
FAMILY-FRIENDLY:	Several old woods roads ideal for young children; be aware of mountain bikers
DOG-FRIENDLY:	On leash

CONTACT/MAP: Kitsap County Parks, www.kitsapgov.com/parks/Parks /Documents/Trail_Maps/nkhp_map.pdf

GPS: N 47 47.078 W 122 32.719

GETTING THERE

Driving: From Kingston, follow State Route 104 west for 2.5 miles. Turn left on Miller Bay Road and continue south for 1.8 miles to the trailhead, on your left.

From Poulsbo, follow SR 307 (Bond Road) east for 2.9 miles, turning right onto Gunderson Road. Continue for 2.3 miles west, turning left onto Miller Bay Road. Continue 1.2 miles north to the trailhead, on your right.

Transit: Kitsap Transit #32 Poulsbo-Silverdale, Kitsap Transit #43 Viking Avenue, and Kitsap Transit #91 Kingston/ Bainbridge, #92 Poulsbo/Kingston Suquamish all stop here.

Established in 2010 and now Kitsap County's third largest park, the North Kitsap Heritage Park forms a huge green wedge between Kingston and Indianola. It is laced with old woods roads and new volunteer-built trails that invite short walks, long hikes, or invigorating runs. You'll be sharing many of these trails with mountain bikers, so keep young children nearby.

Another large protected area purchased through the Kitsap Forest and Bay Project (see sidebar "Kitsap Peninsula First Peoples"), the North Kitsap Heritage Park was recently expanded in 2014, bringing its total area to more than 800 acres. Conservationists recently secured the adjacent 270-acre Grovers Creek Preserve, bringing local trail and conservation advocates closer to their goal of securing a large green swath across the north Kitsap Peninsula—and a cross-peninsula trail with it. But no need to wait for that, as the North Kitsap Heritage Park now has more than 10 miles of trails to explore.

GET MOVING

Where to begin? From beside the old barn with the intriguing mural, of course! From here you can follow the Spine Line (an

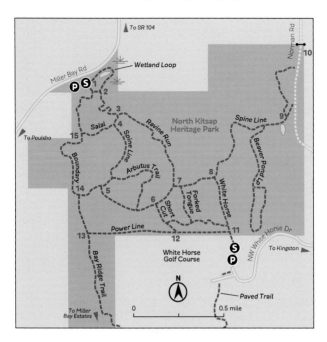

old logging road) to connect with many of the park's other trails. You can make several loops, starting with a very short one leading around the small wetland pools by the barn.

Here's a brief synopsis of the park's trails—mix and match them to meet your mileage requirements.

SPINE LINE leaves the barn and climbs a couple hundred feet through mixed forest. At 1.7 miles it connects with the White Horse Trail and then rapidly descends to cross a small stream and a grassy wetland area. The trail then briefly climbs and bends north, following a road (stay left where another road leads to a treatment plant) terminating at Norman Road at 2.9 miles.

BOUNDARY TRAIL leaves the Spine Line just beyond the wetland pools. The trail utilizes a boardwalk across a wetland area before climbing along the park's western boundary for

Well-signed intersection at North Kitsap Heritage Park

1 mile. Here you can take a short connector to the Spine Line and return to the trailhead for a 2-mile loop—or take the 0.2-mile Salal Trail at 0.4 mile to the Spine Line for a 1-mile loop.

BAY RIDGE TRAIL leaves the Boundary Trail at its southern end and travels 0.9 mile through thick forest to the Miller Bay Estates neighborhood.

POWER LINE TRAIL leaves the Bay Ridge Trail 0.2 mile from the Boundary Trail junction and follows a powerline right-of-way for an up-and-down mile along the park's southern boundary, terminating at the White Horse Trail.

WHITE HORSE TRAIL leaves the Spine Line at 1.7 miles and heads south 0.4 mile before leaving the park and continuing as a paved trail to the White Horse Golf Course, where there is a trailhead with public parking.

RAVINE RUN is a pleasant singletrack trail that leaves the Spine Line at 0.4 mile and reconnects with it at 1.5 miles. It travels for 0.6 mile along a ravine edge, making a little dip and traversing a maple grove. Combined with the Spine Line it makes for a nice 2.5-mile loop.

There are a couple of other marked singletrack trails (consult map) in the park, allowing for more exploring and loop options.

26 Port Gamble Trails

DISTANCE:	More than 60 miles of trails and woods roads
ELEVATION GAIN:	Up to 1000 feet
HIGH POINT:	470 feet
DIFFICULTY:	Easy to moderate
FITNESS:	Walkers, hikers, runners
FAMILY-FRIENDLY:	Beaver Trail and trails near Port Gamble town site are ideal for young children, but be aware of heavy mountain bike use
DOG-FRIENDLY:	On leash
AMENITIES:	Privy
CONTACT/MAP:	Kitsap County Parks, www.kitsapgov.com/parks/Parks /Pages/heritageparks/port_gamble.htm; North Kitsap Trails Association, www.northkitsaptrails.org
GPS:	N47 50.401 W122 35.258
BEFORE YOU GO:	Download and carry a copy of the North Kitsap Trails Association trail map (see website). The Port Gamble Trails host annual running and biking events, so be aware of event closures. Trails outside of the park are subject to closure during periods of extensive drought to protect from fire, and to periodic closures due to logging operations; check website for updates.

A wood-carved pileated woodpecker points the way to North Flicker Road.

GETTING THERE

Driving: From Kingston, follow State Route 104 west for 4 miles to SR 307. Turn right at the light, continuing on SR 104 for 2.7 miles to the county park trailhead (also known as Bay View Trailhead) and parking on the left.

From Poulsbo, follow SR 307 (Bond Road) east for 5.7 miles, turning left at the light onto SR 104. Then follow SR 104 for 2.7 miles to the county park trailhead and parking on the left.

Additional parking and trailheads can be found on Stottlemeyer Road (0.5 mile west of junction with SR 307); on the Port Gamble Road (0.2 mile south of the junction with SR 104); and the Uplands Trailhead near Port Gamble (0.5 mile north of the county park trailhead on SR 104).

Run or hike on more than 60 miles of trails and woods roads traversing more than 3800 acres of timberlands bordering an historic logging community (see sidebar "Puget Sound's

PUGET SOUND'S NEW ENGLAND VILLAGE

Port Gamble is one of Washington's oldest non-Native settlements, and it looks like it came straight out of New England—because in essence, it did! In 1853 Andrew Pope and William Talbot, two Maine lumbermen attracted to the vast forests of the Oregon Territory, formed with partner Josiah Keller and Charles Foster, the Puget Mill Company (eventually becoming Pope and Talbot) at the mouth of Port Gamble.

With a shortage of workers in the territory, they recruited mill workers from East Machias, Maine, to Port Gamble. To accommodate the transplanted workers' homesickness for their New England village, the houses and many other buildings in the new company town of Port Gamble were constructed reflecting the architecture of the buildings back east.

Eventually the mill owners employed members of the S'Klallam tribe from Little Boston across the port. The Puget Sound Mill Company, meanwhile, amassed quite a large amount of the Kitsap and Olympic peninsulas' timberlands. The Port Gamble Mill became a source of lumber for around the world, and the company strongly influenced the industry. This mill would become the longest continuously working lumber mill in North America. When it shut down in 1995, it had been in service for 142 years.

The 1960s marked the beginning of preservation of the company town's numerous residences and commercial buildings. In 1966 Port Gamble was declared a National Historic Landmark, particularly because it represents one of the best examples of a nineteenth-century Pacific Coast logging community, but unique also in containing many buildings constructed with the architecture of a New England village from that period. The oldest house within the district dates to 1859. Stop in at the town's museum to learn more about this fascinating community and the important role Port Gamble played in the economic development of the region and country. And pick up a map and walk around the community discovering its many historic charms and scenic shoreline views.

New England Village"). The Port Gamble Trails are currently the focus of a major conservation initiative to permanently protect this forested block from development, with great potential for a well-planned trail network. But in the meantime, have fun exploring the mishmash of logging roads and user-built routes throughout the forest.

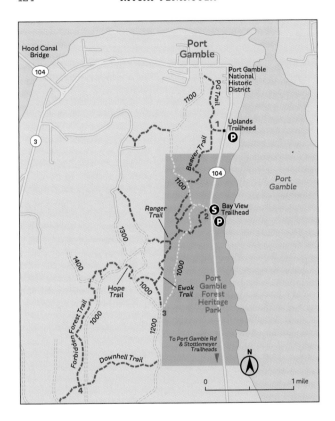

Most of the trails are on a large privately owned tract of land south of Port Gamble that has been in timber production since the 1850s. Olympic Resources Management (ORM), a division of Pope Resources, has graciously allowed the public to passively recreate on their land. However, a few years ago the company decided that it no longer wants to own timberland on the Kitsap Peninsula. Fortunately they have been working with area government officials and conservationists who have shown an interest in purchasing nearly 7000 of the company's Kitsap acres in the hope of keeping them undeveloped and open to public access.

In 2014 Kitsap County Parks secured 535 acres of ORM's Port Gamble tract for a new Port Gamble Forest Heritage Park. This parcel includes wetlands, mature forest, and 1.8 miles of undeveloped shoreline on Port Gamble. Park officials are planning on constructing a top-notch shoreline trail that is sure to become one of the Kitsap Peninsula's premier trails.

GET MOVING

Although most of the Port Gamble Trails will appeal more to mountain bikers (who have built and maintain many of the trails) than to foot travelers, trail runners can put in some serious mileage on some decent terrain here, getting a good workout. Along with mountain bike events, the Port Gamble Trails regularly stage organized trail-running events.

For hikers and walkers, the most appealing routes will be in the northern part of the Port Gamble trail system. The southern half consists of a network of short mountain-bike trails (flowy, banked) through some recent timber-harvest areas. This area is less interesting in terms of natural beauty; there is, however, an old cut area along Road 1700 that offers some decent Olympic mountain views.

Currently almost all of the trails are unmarked, so route-finding can be a challenge. Roads are marked, and there are fifteen location posts with maps scattered around the forest. The map produced by the North Kitsap Trails Association is highly accurate, and you should carry it around with you. There is a lot of territory to explore here, and you can expect some changes over the years. From the county park trailhead, here are some suggested trips for exploring the Port Gamble trails.

BEAVER TRAIL

This is one of the nicest trails for hikers in the Port Gamble system, and it is kid-friendly. From the trailhead, walk Road 1000 for 0.1 mile, turning right onto Road 1100. After another 0.15 mile, locate an unmarked trail to the right. Take it, eventually following a creek, crossing it on a bridge. Then follow a boardwalk along a big beaver pond. At 1 mile from your start you'll come to the Uplands Trailhead (privy and parking), complete with its hobby airplane field.

You can make a loop of about 3 miles by continuing from the Uplands Trailhead on the PG Trail to Port Gamble. Visit the town (see sidebar "Puget Sound's New England") and return to the trailhead via Road 1100.

RANGER TRAIL

Follow Road 1000 for about 0.2 mile to this unmarked trail, which takes off to the right. It leads through young forest interspersed with giant stumps, reminders of the old-growth forest that was logged here long ago. The trail then climbs via a series of short switchbacks to a ridge. It eventually transitions to a mature forest with thick undergrowth. At 0.8 mile you'll reach Road 1200 (elev. 350 feet). Turn left and walk 0.1 mile to Road 1000. Then turn left, and follow this pleasant road mostly downhill for about 1.3 miles back to the trailhead.

FORBIDDEN FOREST

This trail leads through a thick understory of evergreen huckleberry, dipping in and out of a cool little ravine. To reach it, follow Road 1000 for about 1.5 miles (the trail is on right after Road 1300 junction). Then hike this curvy trail for about 1.1 miles to location post 4. From here you can return on Road 1000 or take the Downhell Trail for 0.6 mile to Road 1200. Turn left here and walk 0.3 mile to location post 3 at the junction with Forest Road 1000. Head right, returning to the trailhead in about 1 mile.

GO FARTHER

Trail runners or hikers looking to do a grand run or extended hike at Port Gamble can follow roads and trails along the forest's periphery, for a tally of 15 to 20 miles.

27 Hansville Greenway

DISTANCE:	More than 8 miles of trails
ELEVATION GAIN:	Up to 225 feet
HIGH POINT:	225 feet
DIFFICULTY:	Easy to moderate
FITNESS:	Walkers, hikers, runners
FAMILY-FRIENDLY:	Well-marked and -maintained trail perfect for children of all ages; some trails open to horse and bikes
DOG-FRIENDLY:	On leash
AMENITIES:	Benches, privy, picnic shelter, playground and beach at Buck Lake Park access
CONTACT/MAP:	The Hansville Greenway, http://hansvillegreenway.org
GPS:	N47 54.586 W122 33.315

GETTING THERE

Driving: From Kingston, follow State Route 104 west for 2.5 miles. Turn right onto Hansville Road NE and drive 7.3 miles, turning left onto Buck Lake Road. (For the Norwegian Point Park access, continue beyond the Buck Lake Road junction 0.2 mile north on Hansville Road NE, to the park on your right.) Proceed for 0.8 mile on Buck Lake Road to the Buck Lake County Park entrance. The trailhead is located in the southwest corner of a ballfield. Parking is at the trailhead.

From Poulsbo, follow SR 307 (Bond Road) east for 5.7 miles to SR 104. Continue east on SR 104 for 1.5 miles, turning left onto Hansville Road NE, then follow the directions above.

One of the finest hiking destinations on the Kitsap Peninsula, the Hansville Greenway consists of two tracts of public land comprising over 260 acres and several conservation easements. A network of trails strings these lands together, allowing for extensive hiking. The heart of the greenway is traversed by an old logging railbed-turned-trail leading to several large undeveloped and wildlife-rich bodies of water.

Sid Knutson Puget Sound to Hood Canal Trail

    The Hansville Greenway is an example of what can happen when concerned local citizens come together to work with a governing agency toward a common conservation goal: protecting a wildlife corridor, with opportunities for recreation. In the 1990s the Hansville Greenway Association, along with Kitsap County Parks, began acquiring land for a nature preserve in the relatively undeveloped northern reaches of the peninsula. They then began building trails within this emerging greenway which now extend across the tip of the peninsula from Puget Sound to Hood Canal.

GET MOVING

The trails and junctions are well maintained and marked. Here are three trip suggestions to explore the greenway—feel free to shorten, lengthen, or combine them.

HEART OF THE GREENWAY

Starting from Buck Lake County Park entrance, head through the Welcome Wood to the meadow kiosk (at 0.3 mile). Here at junction 2 head left through Otter Meadow and continue under stately firs, passing Muskrat Swamp. Come to junction 4 at Alder Hollow (at 0.6 mile). Turn left on a wide trail on what was once part of a narrow-gauge logging railway, built in the 1920s and now part of the Sid Knutson Puget Sound to Hood Canal Trail.

Come to junction 5 at 0.7 mile. The trail left leads for 0.3 mile to a planked resting area overlooking Upper Hawks Pond (actually more of a swamp), affectionately called Quiet Place. Continue south on the railroad trail to junction 6 (at 0.8 mile). Head left, skirting wetlands and traversing pleasant woods, to arrive at yet another trail junction 13 (at 1.3 miles). Turn left and head 0.1 mile to Lower Hawks Pond with its beautiful elevated wooden observation platform, perfect for scoping this eutrophic waterway. In addition to the myriad of birds that live in and along this nutrient-rich body of water, look for bear, coyotes, and deer. Return the way you came for a total of 2.8 miles.

SID KNUTSON PUGET SOUND TO HOOD CANAL TRAIL

This is a great 4.1-mile one-way trail that traverses the entire greenway and includes a couple of short road walks. The trail starts at Norwegian Point Park with a short road walk west along Twin Spits Road. At 0.3 mile, pick up the trail and hike south, crossing a wetland on a boardwalk. Walk a short section of gravel Cora Avenue, passing a spur trail heading left (east) to Hansville Road NE.

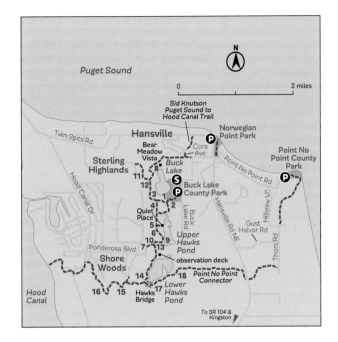

Continue on the road and steadily ascend. At 0.7 mile resume trail walking, passing through groves of mature alders. The way then bends south, climbing some more and reaching junction 8 (elev. 180 feet) at 1.1 miles. Here a short trail leads left to the Bear Meadow Vista. Your route continues south along the greenway boundary demarcating maturing forest and cut-over forest. Pass a spur trail leading to the Sterling Highlands neighborhood, and reach junction 3 at 1.7 miles where the trail straight leads to Buck Lake County Park.

Turn right and continue south on the old logging railbed, passing several junctions and coming to junction 13 at Lower Hawks Pond at 2.6 miles. Continue south along the pond, reaching junction 14 at 2.9 miles. The trail left leads to Point No

Point County Park (see below and Hike 28). You want to continue right, following an old road and passing a spur (junction 15) leading right to the Shore Woods neighborhood.

The trail then descends into a ravine to cross Hawks Hole Creek and comes to junction 16 at 3.4 miles. Here bend right, following along the edge of the ravine and eventually reaching Hood Canal Drive at 4 miles. The trail—now a road walk—heads left 0.1 mile to a junction. Turn right here onto Hood Canal Place, and follow this quiet road downhill, reaching the public beach access on Hood Canal and a splendid view out to the Hood Canal Bridge and the Olympics at 4.1 miles. Rest on the beach before making your return.

POINT NO POINT CONNECTOR

From junction 14 you can take an adventurous hike all the way to Point No Point County Park. Descend into a ravine and cross Hawks Hole Creek on the well-built Hawks Bridge, then reach a logging road at 0.1 mile. Turn left, following the road and returning to the trail (left) at 0.4 mile (junction 18). Now on an easement through thick forest, the trail follows old skid roads, climbing with a few dips along the way. At 1.6 miles, come to Hansville Road NE (elev. 225 feet). Carefully cross it and walk a short distance right (south) along the road to pick up trail once again.

Then descend into a cedar gulch, crossing a creek on a boardwalk. Climb out of the gulch and make a few ups and downs before reaching Thors Road at 2.2 miles. The route is now a road walk. Turn left and walk Thors Road, taking in beautiful views across Puget Sound to the Cascades. At 2.6 miles reach Point No Point County Park (see Hike 28).

From here you can follow the trail through the park for 0.8 mile, then walk 1.1 miles back to Norwegian Point Park via Point No Point Road. Combine this route with the Sid Knutson Puget Sound to Hood Canal Trail for a nearly 10-mile grand loop.

28 Point No Point

DISTANCE:	0.8 mile of trail and nearly 1.5 miles of beach
ELEVATION GAIN:	100 feet
HIGH POINT:	100 feet
DIFFICULTY:	Easy
FITNESS:	Walkers, hikers
FAMILY-FRIENDLY:	Wide, smooth trail and sandy beach perfect for children of all ages
DOG-FRIENDLY:	On leash
AMENITIES:	Privy, picnic tables, interpretive plaques, historic lighthouse and keeper's house
CONTACT/MAP:	The Hansville Greenway, http://hansvillegreenway.org
GPS:	N47 54.717 W122 31.681

GETTING THERE

Driving: From Kingston, follow State Route 104 west for 2.5 miles. Turn right onto Hansville Road NE and drive 7.3 miles, turning right onto Point No Point Road. Proceed for 1.1 miles to Point No Point County Park. Parking here is limited, but you may find overflow parking 0.3 mile west at the public fishing access (Discover Pass required). Parking is also available at Thors Road NE.

From Poulsbo, follow SR 307 (Bond Road) east for 5.7 miles to SR 104. Continue east on SR 104 for 1.5 miles, turning left onto Hansville Road NE; then follow the directions above.

Most folks visit this 60-acre park for its historic lighthouse (the oldest on Puget Sound) and nice stretch of sandy beach granting views of Mounts Baker and Rainier. But a quiet, lovely 0.8-mile trail traverses the property, leading from lighthouse to low dunes to a bluff cloaked with old-growth trees.

The moniker Point No Point was bestowed in 1841 by Commander Charles Wilkes, naming it for a similar spot on the

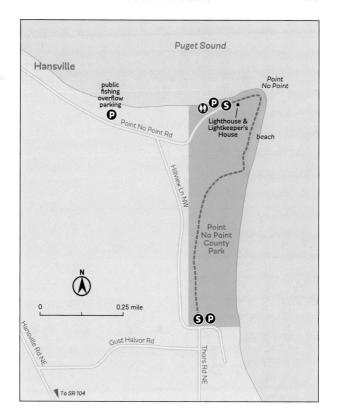

Hudson River. Like that point in New York, this one too appeared and disappeared when viewed from the deck of a ship.

GET MOVING

Start your hike by moseying around the former lightkeeper's home—now a vacation rental and offices for the US Lighthouse Society. Then check out the Point No Point Lighthouse. Built in 1879, it is the oldest lighthouse in Puget Sound. Wander around these grounds and soon learn that there's more than just maritime history associated with this point.

Point No Point Lighthouse

It was here that in 1855, Washington Territorial governor Isaac Stevens and his council convened with tribal leaders of the S'Klallam, Chimakum, and Skokomish tribes to sign the Point No Point Treaty. This treaty, like almost all others between state, territorial, and federal government officials and Native tribes, was less than favorable (putting it politely) for the tribes. Its ratification meant the tribes giving up ancestral lands and being moved to small reservations in exchange for a pittance of a payment. They were, however, allowed to retain some of their hunting and fishing rights.

Continue down the trail, rounding the point. The trail heads south through low-lying dunes covered with grasses and lined with giant driftwood logs.

At 0.2 mile reach an observation deck. The view across Puget Sound to Mount Baker, Three Fingers, Mount Rainier, and the Seattle skyline is breathtaking. Continue south where paths from the main trail invite you to roam the beach. Then climb some stairs to a small bluff, passing a good viewpoint along the way.

The trail then turns inland to follow an old woods road through a grove of old-growth conifers, including some impressive grand firs. At 0.8 mile reach the trail's end at the Thors Road trailhead. From here, retrace your steps back to your car.

GO FARTHER
You can extend your hike by walking either Point No Point Road or Thors Road to trails leading to the Hansville Greenway (see Hike 27 for details).

29 Foulweather Bluff

DISTANCE:	1.9 miles round-trip
ELEVATION GAIN:	Minimal
HIGH POINT:	20 feet
DIFFICULTY:	Easy
FITNESS:	Walkers, hikers
FAMILY-FRIENDLY:	Level, easy trail and a stretch of sandy beach ideal for young children
DOG-FRIENDLY:	Dogs prohibited
CONTACT/MAP:	The Nature Conservancy, www.nature.org /ourinitiatives/regions/northamerica/unitedstates /washington/placesweprotect/foulweather-bluff.xml
GPS:	N47 54.586 W122 33.315
BEFORE YOU GO:	The preserve is open during daylight hours only. Stay on the trail while hiking to the beach; beachcombing is prohibited.

GETTING THERE
Driving: From Kingston, follow State Route 104 west for 2.5 miles. Turn right onto Hansville Road NE and drive 7.5 miles to Hansville where road bends left (west) and becomes Twin Spits Road. Continue on this road for 2.8 miles to the trailhead, on the left (it's easy to miss). Park on the road's shoulder.

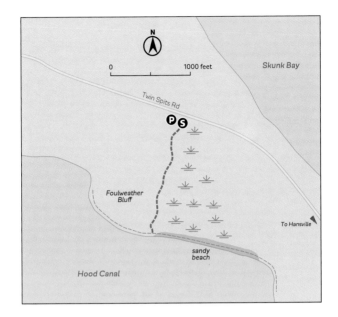

From Poulsbo, follow SR 307 (Bond Road) east for 5.7 miles to SR 104. Continue east on SR 104 for 1.5 miles, turning left onto Hansville Road NE, then follow the directions above.

Hike through a lush band of forest along a large wetland bustling with birdlife to a beautiful strand of Hood Canal beach at the northern tip of the Kitsap Peninsula. One of the best bird-watching spots on the peninsula, Foulweather Bluff is also one of the area's best spots to enjoy a quiet walk and contemplate the beauty of the natural world.

While a little more than 100 acres in size, this Nature Conservancy property is quite diverse, harboring maritime forest, a large brackish wetland, coastal bluffs, and sandy shoreline. With all these distinct habitats, this area is flourishing with wildlife—the reason the Nature Conservancy, one of the largest conservation organizations in America, chose to protect it. You

A group of hikers resting beneath glacial till at Foulweather Bluff

may see bald eagles, osprey, great blue herons, goldeneyes, buffleheads, scoters, wigeons, pigeon guillemots, and murres. Winter is especially a good time to visit when loons, grebes, and scoters are often present in the coastal waters.

GET MOVING

It's just a 0.3-mile level walk to the beach, but the beach offers much to explore. Plan on spending some time here, and aim for a low tide so that you can walk the full kilometer (0.6 mile) of beach from end to end, binoculars and bird guide in hand.

The trail delivers you to the beach at its midpoint. So, you'll want to do two out-and-backs from this point. Interestingly, it'll be like walking in two very different areas. The beach north is strewn with rocks and hemmed in by a towering bluff of glacial till with madronas dangling on its rim. Within the rocky bluff face are plenty of burrows, home to nesting birds.

The beach south from the trail is a sandy barrier protecting the marsh from Hood Canal. It's a gorgeous stretch of shoreline—one of the finest little beaches on the peninsula.

Be sure that you turn around at the preserve's boundaries, respecting the private property beyond.

Next page: Mount Rainier seen from Pritchard Park

BAINBRIDGE ISLAND

Kitsap County's Bainbridge Island (population around 23,000) sits in the heart of Puget Sound. Connected to the Kitsap Peninsula by a bridge and to Seattle by ferry, many a resident commutes to the city for work. Although the entire island is incorporated as a city, much of Bainbridge is semi-rural with large tracts of parks and preserves. If ever there was a community in the Northwest that felt like it could be in Connecticut, Bainbridge Island is it, with upscale residential areas, a quaint downtown business district, horse farms, and an extensive park and trail network.

Thanks to the very active Bainbridge Island Land Trust, the island has preserved a remarkably large amount of land for parks, preserves, and trails despite the development pressures. Most of these parks and trails are managed by the Bainbridge Island Metropolitan Park and Recreation District (BIMPRD)—and along with a large contingent of dedicated volunteers, they oversee some of the best-marked and -maintained trails in the Northwest. City officials, conservation leaders, and active citizens are working hard toward having an interconnecting trail system in place traversing much of the island.

30 Fort Ward Park

DISTANCE:	2 miles round-trip
ELEVATION GAIN:	140 feet
HIGH POINT:	140 feet
DIFFICULTY:	Easy to moderate
FITNESS:	Walkers, hikers, runners
FAMILY-FRIENDLY:	Paved trail and wide, well-graded trail through old military installation; paved trails ADA-accessible
DOG-FRIENDLY:	On leash
AMENITIES:	Privies, picnic tables, water, Cascadia Marine Trail campsites
CONTACT/MAP:	Bainbridge Island Metro Park & Recreation District, www.biparks.org/biparks_site/parks/fortward.htm
GPS:	N47 35.342 W122 31.897
BEFORE YOU GO:	The park is open from 8:00 AM to dusk.

GETTING THERE

Driving: From the Bainbridge Island Ferry Terminal, follow State Route 305 north for 1 mile, turning left onto High School Road. (From SR 3 in Poulsbo, follow SR 305 south for 12.5 miles, turning right onto High School Road.) Continue west for 2 miles, then turn left onto Fletcher Bay Road. Drive 1.3 miles and turn right onto Lynwood Center Road. Continue 1.1 miles, turning left onto Pleasant Beach Drive. Follow this road for 1.3 miles (be sure to bear right at 0.7 mile) to the Fort Ward park entrance and northern trailhead with parking. The park's eastern trailhead and parking (seasonal) are accessed from Fort Ward Hill Road NE.

Transit: Kitsap Transit route #98 Fort Ward accesses the eastern trailhead.

Built in 1903 to protect the Bremerton Naval Shipyard, Fort Ward was decommissioned in 1958. Soon afterward it became a state park, eventually transferred to the BIMPRD. While the historic fort's two batteries attract plenty of interest, its 4300

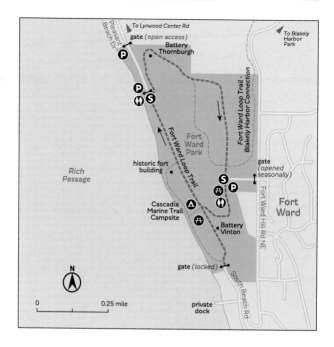

feet of gorgeous shoreline on Rich Passage and old-growth forest are the real attraction here.

GET MOVING

The best way to enjoy the 137-acre park is to hike its 2-mile loop. (If you're interested in just walking along the shoreline, proceed straight on the former road, now a paved trail.) For the loop, locate a wide track taking off northwest into a forested bluff. Curving northeast under a canopy of stately old trees, you soon come to Battery Thornburgh. The strategic view across Rich Passage to the former defense installation at Manchester State Park is now blocked by over a half century of greenery. The battery sports some graffiti but still warrants a look-see; interpretive panels help you understand its past function.

A hiker enjoying the view across Rich Passage

Continue on the wide trail, steadily ascending and coming to a junction at 0.3 mile. The trail branching right meets back up with the loop in about 0.4 mile, offering an alternative route. The main loop continues left through a forest of big maples and firs. As over much of Bainbridge Island, the forest floor here has been taken over by invasive ivy. At 0.7 mile reach a four-way junction. The trail right is the other end of the alternative route. The trail left is a quiet 1.2-mile trail that travels through old cedars and along a lush creek bed to Blakely Harbor Park.

For the loop, continue straight, soon reaching the eastern parking lot and trailhead. Pick up a paved path at the south end of the lot and steeply descend. Bear right where a path heads left to Fort Ward Hill Road and to the former fort residences (now privately owned, but feel free to walk the neighborhood, admiring the structures from the roads).

At 1.2 miles reach the paved former road-trail. The loop continues right, but first you may want to head left (south) and walk the road-trail 0.2 mile to its end at a residential development. This section of the trail will take you to the old fort's other battery, Battery Vinton, and to a parallel shoreline path.

To complete the loop, head right and follow the wide and shaded old road trail—or better yet, follow the road trail and divert onto the two short paralleling shoreline paths. The two paths tunnel through rows of Nootka rose and hawthorn and traverse open bluffs along Rich Passage, granting exceptional views and bird-watching. As you walk above the shoreline, look for cormorants perched on a piling.

Mosey across the open fort fields and past a couple of restored buildings. At about 2 miles you'll return to your start at the northwestern parking lot.

GO FARTHER

The 1.2-mile Fort Ward Blakely Harbor Trail is a pleasant hike. From the junction noted above (where the alternate route reenters the main loop) just north of the park's eastern trailhead, the trail steadily descends alongside a small creek in a ravine of thick mature timber. The trail terminates (parking available) on Country Club Road near its junction with Blakely Avenue. Across Country Club Road you can walk on the emerging trail system in the 40-acre Blakely Harbor Park. Once the site of the Port Blakely Mill, one of the largest sawmills in the 1890s, this beautiful little park offers a large dose of history as well with its scenic shoreline trails. BIMPRD is currently building trails and interpretive displays at this fairly new park.

31 Gazzam Lake Nature Preserve

DISTANCE:	4 miles of trails
ELEVATION GAIN:	Up to 400 feet
HIGH POINT:	385 feet
DIFFICULTY:	Easy to moderate
FITNESS:	Hikers, runners
FAMILY-FRIENDLY:	Trails to lake are wide and gentle, suitable for young children; some trails open to bikes and horses
DOG-FRIENDLY:	On leash
CONTACT/MAP:	Bainbridge Island Metro Park & Recreation District, www.biparks.org/biparks_site/parks/gazzam-lake.htm
GPS:	N47 37.489 W122 33.961

GETTING THERE

Driving: From the Bainbridge Island Ferry Terminal, follow State Route 305 north for 1 mile, turning left onto High School Road. (From SR 3 in Poulsbo, follow SR 305 south for 12.5 miles, turning right onto High School Road.) Continue west for 2 miles and turn left onto Fletcher Bay Road NE. Drive 0.4 mile, turning right onto Island Center Road NE. Then drive 0.8 mile and turn right onto Marshall Road. Proceed 0.4 mile to the trailhead.

For the Deerpath (southern) trailhead, from High School Road continue 1.3 miles on Fletcher Bay Road, turning right onto Lynwood Center Road. Then drive 1 mile, turning right onto Baker Hill Road. Continue 0.8 mile and turn right onto gravel Deerpath Lane. Proceed 0.2 mile to the trailhead.

Transit: Kitsap Transit route #97 Crystal Springs accesses Deerpath Lane, from where it's a short walk to the preserve's southern trailhead.

Go for a short leisurely walk or an all-day jaunt in this 440-acre preserve, which includes a 13-acre undeveloped lake, mature forest, and secluded beach on Port Orchard Narrows. The largest protected tract and second largest undeveloped area on the island, this heavily forested property is traversed by 4 miles of well-developed trails, with new ones in the works.

Through bond sales, grants, donations, and support from the Bainbridge Island Land Trust, the Gazzam Lake Nature Preserve continues to grow. And through the help of dedicated volunteers, the preserve's trail system continues to grow as well.

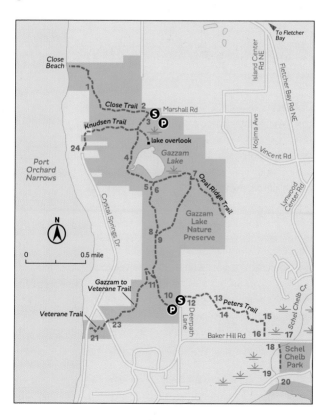

Serene Gazzam Lake

GET MOVING

From the Marshall Road trailhead, follow an old road (now a wide trail) 0.1 mile through attractive woods to a junction. (All junctions are marked with numbered posts.) From here you can head left for Gazzam Lake or right for Close Beach.

For Close Beach, continue on the road and, after cresting a small hill, begin descending. The trail leaves the old woods road for singletrack and then steeply descends (at times with the aid of steps) into a lush ravine. Marvel at some large Douglas firs that escaped the ax—and notice plenty of invasive holly that needs to be axed from the landscape.

At 0.7 mile from the junction, reach a secluded little cobbled beach on Port Orchard Narrows. If the tide is low, wander about; if it's high, admire the Sound waters from beneath a canopy of shoreline cedars. Look across the narrows to Illahee State Park, and up the narrows to Keyport.

For Gazzam Lake, head left on an old road, soon passing the new Knudsen Trail which heads 0.6 mile to Crystal Springs Drive. At 0.25 mile from the junction, come to a spur leading to the lake. The little lake, named after a prominent early resident of the island, is surrounded by big firs and cedars and ringed with lily pads and reeds. A nice gap in the vegetation allows you to sit and watch for avian and mammalian residents.

From the lake spur, the trail continues south, passing another lake-access spur and coming to a junction 0.5 mile from the Close Beach Trail junction. You can go left here and return right for an easy 1-mile loop that crosses a small meadow. A singletrack trail, the Opal Ridge Trail, diverts from this loop. This quiet little trail travels 0.3 mile through attractive forest (but no ridge) to private property.

You can skip the loop and just continue right on the old road for 0.8 mile to the Deerpath Lane trailhead. En route you'll pass a couple of pocket meadows (eradicated of invasive species), some big bigleaf maples, and a pair of water towers. You'll also pass the new Gazzam to Veterane Trail leading 0.9 mile west to Crystal Springs Drive.

From the Deerpath Lane trailhead, the hiker-only Peters Trail traverses more preserve property and an easement on the Peters Tree Farm. Among the easement stipulations is that hikers on the trail turn off their cell phones and electronic devices to preserve the quiet of the area. (An interesting concept—and one I suppose many solace-seekers can embrace.)

The Peters Trail heads east on downward route, losing 300 feet of elevation. This pleasant path takes you over a small ravine and through a couple of groves of big trees before terminating in 0.7 mile on Listening Road (private road/no parking). You can continue walking by following this narrow paved road right for 0.15 mile to Baker Hill Road.

Carefully cross the road and walk left a couple of hundred feet to a trail paralleling Schel Chelb Creek. Then follow this pleasant path along the creek for 0.2 mile to Schel Chelb Park on Point White Drive, and a beautiful stretch of public beach on a cove on Rich Passage.

32 Pritchard Park

DISTANCE:	1.2 miles round-trip
ELEVATION GAIN:	40 feet
HIGH POINT:	40 feet
DIFFICULTY:	Easy
FITNESS:	Walkers
FAMILY-FRIENDLY:	Easy trail to sandy beach on Eagle Harbor; watch young children around the old mill area
DOG-FRIENDLY:	On leash
AMENITIES:	Privy, benches, memorial
CONTACT/MAP:	Bainbridge Island Metro Park and Recreation District, www.biparks.org/biparks_site/parks/pritchard.htm
GPS:	N47 36.936 W122 30.529

GETTING THERE

Driving: From the Bainbridge Island Ferry Terminal, follow State Route 305 north for 1 mile, turning left onto High School Road. (From SR 3 in Poulsbo, follow SR 305 south for 12.5 miles, turning right onto High School Road.) Continue west for 0.2 mile, turning left at a roundabout onto Madison Avenue. Drive south 0.5 mile, turning right onto Wyatt Way. Now continue 0.8 mile west on Wyatt Way, which bends left to become Eagle Harbor Drive. Continue on Eagle Harbor Drive, bearing left at 0.2 mile, and drive 2 more miles, turning left into the park.

Transit: Kitsap Transit #99 Bill Point (weekdays only) will stop at the park if you request it.

This former industrial area has a long history, but the city of Bainbridge Island is working hard to transform it into a legacy park. Pritchard Park contains nearly 1 mile of sandy beach and some of the finest views of the Seattle skyline seen from land. It is also home to the Japanese-American Exclusion Memorial, a national historical site marking a somber epoch in American history (see sidebar, "Let It Not Happen Again").

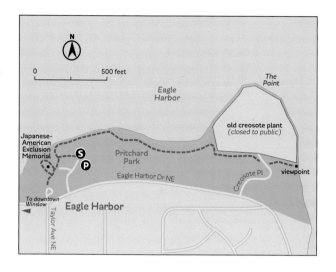

This 50-acre parcel of land is quite significant to Bainbridge Island and to the nation's history. Ancestral home to Salish peoples, in modern times this spot was for many years the site of the village of Creosote and its creosote mill. On the park's western boundary is the old Eagle Harbor ferry landing where Bainbridge Island's Japanese-Americans (the first of the 120,000 folks of Japanese descent in America) were sent to internment camps during World War II.

The area's transformation to a park is still in process. Parts of the park are still closed to visitors (while environmental cleanup proceeds), and the trails lacing the park's uplands (and shown on maps) are primitive and can't yet be recommended for hiking. But the park's Japanese-American Memorial, a fine stretch of beach, and a 0.6-mile hiking route to a scenic viewpoint are definitely worth visiting now.

In case you're wondering, the park takes its name from Joel Pritchard, a longtime GOP statesman from Seattle who served as state lieutenant governor and as a US congressman. Around these parts, he may be better known as one of

Pritchard Park provides excellent views of the Seattle skyline.

the founders of pickleball. Back in 1965, Pritchard and friends Bill Bell and Barney McCallum devised the game from improvisation and ingenuity.

GET MOVING

Start on the wide trail (a former service road), heading west and descending from bluff to beach. Pass a trail leading to the Japanese-American Exclusion Memorial and bend east, emerging upon an inviting sandy beach. Enjoy good views across Eagle Harbor to Winslow (downtown Bainbridge) with busy ferries plying harbor waters to and from Seattle.

Continue walking east, and you'll come to The Point (Bill Point), where from 1904 to 1988 the creosote plant operated. Now a Superfund cleanup site, The Point and its sandy beaches are currently closed until hazardous material can be removed from the soil and more of the old factory removed.

Continue your hike east, following the old access road to a singletrack running alongside the fence surrounding the old factory. The uplands to your right, now covered in thick vegetative growth, once supported the creosote factory's

LET IT NOT HAPPEN AGAIN

Occupying 8 acres of Pritchard Park near the former Eagledale Ferry Dock is the Bainbridge Island Japanese-American Exclusion Memorial (www.bijac.org), commemorating one of the darkest periods in American history. Shortly after the Japanese bombing of Pearl Harbor on December 7, 1941 bringing the United States into World War II, President Franklin Roosevelt signed Executive Order 9066 resulting in the relocation and internment of nearly 120,000 Japanese-Americans from their homes on the West Coast. Allowed to take only a few possessions, these people, many of whom were American citizens, were ushered onto trains and taken to ten internment camps.

The Japanese community on Bainbridge Island was well established at this time, with the first immigrants arriving in the 1880s. Many were engaged in strawberry farming and working at local sawmills. Because of the island's close proximity to the Bremerton shipyards, the Japanese here were the first in the country to be interned. On March 30, 1942, 227 Japanese-Americans departed the island by ferry to awaiting trains in Seattle. From there they were sent to camp in Manzanar, California—and later to Minidoka, Idaho, both harsh desert environments. This somber period was captured well in Bainbridge Island author David Guterson's novel (and later film) *Snow Falling on Cedars*.

This act was a clear violation of these people's constitutional rights under the fourth, fifth, sixth, and fourteenth amendments. The US government wouldn't officially recognize this injustice and apologize for it until President Reagan signed the Civil Liberties Act of 1988. On May 8, 2008, President George W. Bush signed a bill making the Bainbridge Island Japanese-American Exclusion Memorial a national park unit, administered as part of the Minidoka National Historic Site.

Take time to visit and reflect at this outdoor memorial. An organizing group, the Bainbridge Japanese-American Community, plans to eventually build a 4000-square-foot interpretive center on the site. Currently you can follow a beautiful curving boardwalk trail to the cedar story wall, which has the names of all 276 Japanese-American residents on the island at the time. The wall was designed by local award-winning architect Johnpaul Jones. He also worked on the landscape architecture of the memorial, using natural landscaping principles integrating native species. Seattle artist Steve Gardner created the friezes on the wall, depicting scenes of the residents' lives during this time. The memorial's unifying theme is *Nidoto Nai Yoni*, "Let it not happen again."

company town. When you get to Creosote Place (an alternative trailhead), cross the road and continue on a small path to the viewpoint. From the bench on a bluff, take in the superb views of the Seattle skyline; the view of Mount Rainier isn't too shabby either. Stay to watch late-day sunlight and shadows dance across the water.

33 Grand Forest Park

DISTANCE:	8 miles of trails
ELEVATION GAIN:	Up to 500 feet
HIGH POINT:	350 feet
DIFFICULTY:	Easy to moderate
FITNESS:	Hikers, runners
FAMILY-FRIENDLY:	Well-maintained and -marked trail system with easy loop options; several trails open to horses and bicycles
DOG-FRIENDLY:	On leash
CONTACT/MAP:	Bainbridge Island Metro Park and Recreation District, www.biparks.org/biparks_site/parks/grand-forest.htm
GPS:	N47 39.410 W122 33.634

GETTING THERE

Driving: From the Bainbridge Island Ferry Terminal, follow State Route 305 north for 1.6 miles, turning left onto Madison Avenue. In 0.1 mile turn right onto New Brooklyn Road and proceed for 2.1 miles, turning right onto Miller Road. Continue north 1 mile to the trailhead, on your right. Parking is at the trailhead.

(From Poulsbo, follow SR 305 south, turning right onto Day Road. The turnoff is located 2 miles south of Agate Pass Bridge. Then immediately bear left onto Miller Road and proceed for 1.8 miles to the trailhead, on your left.)

Trailheads with parking can also be found on Mandus Olson Road on both the north and south side of the forest.

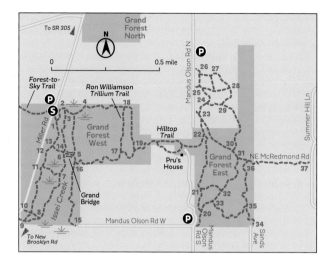

Transit: Kitsap Transit Route #106 Fletcher Bay (weekdays only) goes to Tolo Road, where the park can be accessed at trail waypoint 11.

Grand indeed, this large park—consisting of three contiguous parcels totaling over 240 acres—is many a Bainbridge Islander's favorite local place to hike and run. A well-designed and meticulously maintained network of trails allows for lots of loop options. And the forest—consisting of mature evergreens, ferny gulches, babbling brooks, and wetland pools—will leave you feeling like you're deep in a faraway wilderness.

Formerly two separate parcels, Grand Forest West and Grand Forest East were recently connected via the Hilltop parcel thanks to the Bainbridge Island Land Trust. The 4-mile in-the-works Cross Island Trail (CIT) threads together all three parcels, allowing for long hikes and runs. Grand Forest West is definitely the busiest of the three parcels. If you're interested in just visiting Grand Forest East, you can access this parcel from trailheads off the Mandus Olson Road.

Meadows on the Hilltop within the Grand Forest

GET MOVING

The 8-mile trail system within the park is well marked with waypoint posts at nearly all intersections, numbered from 1 to 37. On several of the posts, you will also see CIT markers and 5K markers. The 5K markers denote a 5K training route (a popular running race distance) utilizing trails in the park and the Forest-to-Sky Trail to Battle Point Park.

The Cross Island Trail (CIT) starts on a small beach north of Battle Point Park and runs through that park. From there it utilizes the Forest-to-Sky Trail and traverses Grand Forest via several trails including the new Hilltop Trail. The CIT then heads east, going through Grand Forest East and following a 0.3-mile corridor to NE McRedmond Road, from there following roads to Manitou Beach.

The 1.5-mile section of the CIT in the Grand Forest begins by soon crossing Issei Creek (named for the island's first generation of Japanese immigrants) on the Grand Bridge. It then skirts a wetland pool before climbing the Hilltop. You may want to pause here on this open grassy hill (elev. 350 feet) to take in views of the surrounding countryside and Olympic Mountains. A new 0.25-mile loop circles the open hilltop, passing old apple trees and Pru's House, a refurbished cabin available for rent by the park's department. The CIT then cuts across the Grand Forest East and steeply descends to NE McRedmond Road.

A nice kid-friendly hike in the Grand Forest West is the 1.2-mile Main Loop, following waypoint posts 1 through 13. It follows alongside Issei Creek, crosses the Grand Bridge, and visits some of the grandest trees in the Grand Forest. The 0.2-mile Ron Williamson Trillium Trail is another favorite, especially in the spring, traveling alongside a large wetland. This trail can be part of several loops.

In the Grand Forest East, the Main Loop trail there follows waypoints 20 through 33 and involves some rolling terrain over a course of about 1.6 miles. Of course, half the fun here is creating your own loops by utilizing the various connector trails.

GO FARTHER

Follow the Forest-to-Sky Trail (starts on the west side of Miller Road across from the main trailhead—use caution crossing road), which is also part of the Cross Island Trail and a marked 5K running route, for 0.9 mile to Battle Point Park. This well-developed and marked trail travels mainly through forest and includes a few ups and downs, crossing a creek via a bridge and a swampy area via a boardwalk. There are a few big trees along the way, and it's an overall pleasant route suitable for hikers of all ages.

There is also a Grand Forest North, a 39-acre noncontiguous tract (accessed from Miller Road) with a small loop trail. The Bainbridge Island Land Trust is currently working on a campaign to connect this parcel with Grand Forest West.

34 Battle Point Park Loop

DISTANCE:	1.6 miles round-trip
ELEVATION GAIN:	Minimal
HIGH POINT:	140 feet
DIFFICULTY:	Easy
FITNESS:	Walkers, runners
FAMILY-FRIENDLY:	Soft-surface groomed trail, perfect for jogging strollers
DOG-FRIENDLY:	On leash
AMENITIES:	Restrooms, water, playfields and tennis courts, picnic shelter
CONTACT/MAP:	Bainbridge Island Metro Park and Recreation District, www.biparks.org/biparks_site/parks /battlepoint.htm ; no map available online
GPS:	N47 39.787 W122 34.530

GETTING THERE

Driving: From the Bainbridge Island Ferry Terminal, follow State Route 305 north for 3 miles, turning left onto Koura Road. Continue west on Koura Road for 1.4 miles, turning left on Miller Road. Proceed for 0.2 mile, turning right onto Arrow Point Drive. (From Poulsbo, follow SR 305 south, turning right onto Day Road; the turnoff is located 2 miles south of Agate Pass Bridge. Then immediately bear left onto Miller Road and proceed for 1.5 miles, turning right onto Arrow Point Drive.) Continue on Arrow Point Drive for 1 mile to the park's east entrance. There are also parking and trail access points on the park's north and west boundaries.

Transit: Kitsap Transit Route #95-Battle Point (weekdays only) stops at all of the park's entrances.

A former naval radar station, Battle Point Park is one of Bainbridge Island's loveliest and busiest parks. A wide and

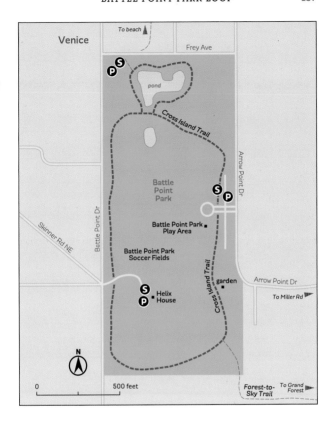

smooth trail travels the park's periphery, traversing open space and skirting the park's happening developed attractions. Highlights along the way are two ponds with abundant birdlife, rows of cottonwoods, and a placid atmosphere.

GET MOVING

From the parking area, access the Battle Point walking trail and go left or right. Going right (counterclockwise) around the loop, here's what you are in store for (if you go left, expect the same in reverse):

Runner on Battle Point Park's loop trail

The wide, hard-packed trail soon intersects with a paved trail, which heads south along the park's eastern boundary, eventually connecting with the Forest-to-Sky Trail (see below).

The loop continues north, coming to a junction near a pond. The trail left shortens the loop by skipping the pond, but the pond is one of the park's best features, so go right, hugging the shoreline of the cottonwood-lined pond—a favorite fishing hole for area children.

You'll soon come to a junction. The trail branching right is a continuation of the Cross Island Trail (which includes part of the main loop trail) leading to the north parking lot. It then crosses Frey Avenue, and picking up again a short distance east to follow a narrow trail corridor to a small beach access on the sound.

The park loop continues south, soon intersecting with the shortcut. The trail then traverses manicured grounds, skirting playfields bustling with youth sports teams. The park occasionally bustles with school cross-country runners as well, so be mindful if you stumble into a competition.

Pass lots of stately ornamental trees and cross the west park access road. Then bend east and intersect with the Forest-to-Sky Trail (part of the Cross Island Trail), which leads to the Grand Forest (see Hike 33). The park loop then heads north, skirting a big community garden to the right and a playground on your left. And by now you certainly have noticed the Helix House in the center of the park. This former part of the radar station now serves as the Battle Point Astronomical Association's planetarium and astronomy center. It's worth a visit after your walk.

GO FARTHER

From Battle Point Park you can follow the Forest-to-Sky Trail, which is also part of the Cross Island Trail and a marked 5K running route to the Grand Forest. This 0.9-mile trail, well marked and developed, travels mainly through forest and includes a few ups and downs, crossing a creek via bridge and a swampy area via boardwalk. There are a few big trees along the way, and it's an overall pleasant route suitable for hikers of all ages.

35   Manzanita Trails

DISTANCE:	2 miles of trails
ELEVATION GAIN:	Up to 100 feet
HIGH POINT:	140 feet
DIFFICULTY:	Easy
FITNESS:	Hikers, runners
FAMILY-FRIENDLY:	Heavily used by equestrians and not suitable for small children
DOG-FRIENDLY:	On leash, and keep dogs well controlled around equestrians

CONTACT/MAP: Bainbridge Island Metro Park and Recreation District,
               www.biparks.org/biparks_site/parks/manzanita.htm;
               no map available online
       GPS: N47 40.979 W122 32.887

GETTING THERE

Driving: From the Bainbridge Island Ferry Terminal, follow State Route 305 for 4.3 miles, turning left onto Day Road. (From Poulsbo, follow SR 305 south. The turnoff is 2 miles south of Agate Pass Bridge.) Continue west on Day Road (being sure to bear right at the Miller Road junction) for 0.4

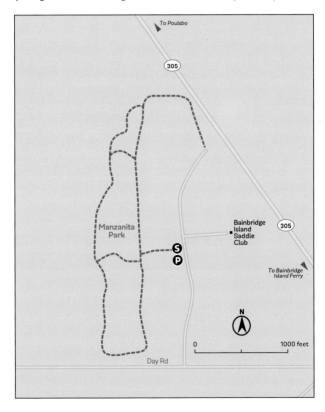

Cedar forest at Manzanita Park

mile, turning right onto the gravel road into Manzanita Park. Proceed for 0.2 mile to the parking area.

Bordering the Bainbridge Island Saddle Club, Manzanita Park is primarily used by equestrians. Hiking is not discouraged here, though, and the trails at times are quiet and devoid of users four and two legged. Just beware of the big beasties on the trails, and consider a late-summer or early-fall visit when the trails are dry and free of mud.

When running and hiking around horses, remember the big equines have the right-of-way. Upon their approach, step to the side of the trail—preferably on the downhill side—and talk to the rider in a calm voice. And remember, if you have your pooch with you, to keep him under control.

GET MOVING

The main access trail starts just south of the parking area. Take this wide path west for 0.1 mile, climbing slightly to a wide trail running north-to-south along a small ridge. This old woods road connects to a paralleling trail, linked by several short trails. Follow the woods road to the parallel trail for a pleasant 1-mile loop.

Runners will enjoy doing repeats on the loop with its several dipsy-dos—and you can add a short uphill sprint or downhill blast by veering onto a loop connector or two.

There are lots of horse jumps along the main loop, although it looks like many haven't been in use since Seattle Slew won the Triple Crown. From the perimeter loop another trail veers east, eventually bending south and leading to the saddle club.

36 West Port Madison Nature Trail

DISTANCE:	0.6 mile round-trip
ELEVATION GAIN:	Minimal
HIGH POINT:	60 feet
DIFFICULTY:	Easy
FITNESS:	Walkers
FAMILY-FRIENDLY:	Easy hike for all ages; keep children away from bluff at trail's end
DOG-FRIENDLY:	On leash
AMENITIES:	Picnic shelter
CONTACT/MAP:	Bainbridge Island Metro Park and Recreation District, www.biparks.org/biparks_site/parks /westportmadison.htm; no map available online
GPS:	N47 42.286 W122 32.295

Rustic picnic shelter

GETTING THERE

Driving: From the Bainbridge Island Ferry Terminal, follow State Route 305 for 5.1 miles, turning right onto West Port Madison Road. (From Poulsbo, follow SR 305. The turnoff is 1.2 miles south of Agate Pass Bridge.) Continue 1.1 miles on West Port Madison Road to the trailhead, located on your left. Parking is at the trailhead.

While only 13 acres in size, this small preserve borders the private-but-open-to-the-public 150-acre Bloedel Reserve, so it feels much bigger. And unlike its popular neighbor, the nature center is free to enter and free of tour buses. Amble through old-growth forest to a pair of rustic picnic shelters. Take along the basket and stay awhile.

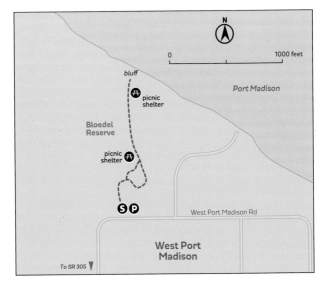

GET MOVING

Follow the wide, soft-surfaced trail into a grove of towering old timber. There are some impressive western red cedars and Douglas firs in this small nature center. In less than 0.1 mile, come to a junction. The two trails meet up again shortly afterward, so either way will do. But the trail left is far more attractive, crossing a bridge over a ferny swale.

Near where the two trails rejoin is the first of two rustic picnic shelters, complete with stone fireplaces. The second shelter is located farther along, near the end of the trail on a bluff. Here you'll get a window view out at Port Madison. Be sure to keep children and dogs away from the bluff's edge. Hang out at the shelter for a while and enjoy the soothing sounds of nature.

GO FARTHER

The nearby Bloedel Reserve (www.bloedelreserve.org) is definitely worth a visit. You can spend all day here walking on trails through the reserve's manicured grounds, gardens, and natural areas. Also nearby consider taking a hike or trail run on the BIMPRD's Hidden Cove Trail system. While this 2-mile trail network mainly weaves through a residential area, many of the homes are well hidden from the trail. You can access the trails from the Hidden Cove Ballfields, located off Phelps Road (north of Day Road off SR 305), adding a pleasant 1-mile round-trip from the ballfields to Hidden Cove Park.

RESOURCES

TRAIL AND CONSERVATION ORGANIZATIONS

Bainbridge Island Land Trust
www.bi-landtrust.org

Forterra
http://forterra.org/

Great Peninsula Conservancy
www.greatpeninsula.org

Kitsap Forest & Bay Project
www.kitsapforestbay.org

Leave No Trace
www.lnt.org

The Mountaineers
www.mountaineers.org

Nature Conservancy
www.nature.org

Opposite: A serene scene at Poulsbo's Fish Park

North Kitsap Trails Association
www.northkitsaptrails.org

Peninsula Wilderness Club
www.pwckitsap.org

Washington State Parks Foundation
http://wspf.org

Washington Trails Association
www.wta.org

ORGANIZED RUNS, HIKES, AND WALKS IN KITSAP

Bainbridge Island Turkey Trot
Family fun run and walk at Battle Point Park
http://bainbridgeturkeytrot.org

Hotfoot 5K Trail Race
www.hotfoot5K.com

Kitsap Volkssporters Walking Club
Active walking group that hosts numerous events
www.kitsapvolkssporters.org

The Mountaineers
Seattle-based outdoors club has a Kitsap Branch involved
with local conservation issues as well as coordinating group
outdoor activities
www.mountaineers.org /kitsap

Peninsula Wilderness Club
Large and active club coordinates group hikes, runs, and pad-
dling events locally and throughout the state
www.pwckitsap.org

Roots Rock Trail Running Race
Trail-running series held on the Port Gamble Trails
http://poulsborunning.com

ACKNOWLEDGMENTS

Researching and writing *Urban Trails: Kitsap* was fun, gratifying, and a lot of hard work. I couldn't have finished this project without the help and support of the following people. A huge thank-you to all the great people at Mountaineers Books; especially publisher, Helen Cherullo, editor-in-chief, Kate Rogers, managing editor Margaret Sullivan, and project editor Nancy Cortelyou.

A big thank-you to my editor Jane Crosen for her attention to detail and thoughtful suggestions that helped to make this book a finer volume. Thanks to Miguel Galeana of Route 16 Running and Walking for first introducing me to the great parks of Gig Harbor. And thanks too, to Mark Mauren of Ueland Tree Farm for taking time to meet and show me around.

I also want to thank my family: wife Heather, son Giovanni, and parents Richard and Judy, for accompanying me on several of the trails in this book. And I thank God for watching over me and keeping me safe and healthy while I hiked and ran all over the Kitsap Peninsula.

INDEX

Opposite: Penrose Point State Park's saltwater shoreline

ABOUT THE AUTHOR

CRAIG ROMANO grew up in rural New Hampshire where he fell in love with the natural world. He moved to Washington in 1989 and has since hiked more than 18,000 miles in the Evergreen State. An avid runner as well, Craig has run more than twenty-five marathons and ultra runs, including the Boston Marathon and the White River 50-Mile Endurance Run.

An award-winning author and co-author of sixteen books, Craig also writes for numerous publications, tourism websites, and Hikeoftheweek.com. His book *Columbia Highlands: Exploring Washington's Last Frontier* was recognized in 2010 by Washington Secretary of State Sam Reed and State Librarian Jan Walsh as a "Washington Reads" book for its contribution to the state's cultural heritage.

When not hiking, running, and writing, Craig can be found napping with his wife, Heather, son, Giovanni, and cats, Giuseppe and Mazie, at his home in Skagit County. Visit him at http://CraigRomano.com and on Facebook at "Craig Romano Guidebook Author."

OTHER TITLES YOU MIGHT ENJOY FROM MOUNTAINEERS BOOKS

Urban Cycling: How to Get to Work, Save Money, and Use Your Bike for City Living
Madi Carlson
Accessible and encouraging advice
for city cyclists

**Fit by Nature: The AdventX
Twelve-Week Outdoor Fitness Program**
John Colver and Nicole Nazzaro
A comprehensive exercise and
lifestyle program—no equipment needed!

**The Healthy Back Book
The Healthy Knees Book**
Astrid Pujari and Nancy Alton
A whole-body approach to injury
prevention and healing

**Yoga for Hikers: How to Stretch,
Strengthen, and Hike Farther**
Nicole Tsong
Easy-to understand poses and
sequences tailored for hikers

**Triathlon Revolution: Training,
Technique, and Inspiration**
Terri Schneider
Complete information for triathlon preparation

www.mountaineersbooks.org